Confessions from a **HELL BOUND TAXI**

Book 1: *Introduction to the Real World*

Special Edition

ISBN 978-0-9833829-1-1

Confessions

from a

HELL
BOUND
TAXI

Book 1: **Introduction to the Real World**

by

Alaric von Boerner

Published by
Ragnaroc Productions
P.O. Box 88
Stockton, California
95201

In a sea of lies the truth will rise up like a serpents head.

To those who have fallen prey to deception,

the truth will appear as a monster.

-- Anonymous

Driving taxi is like being a spy without a cause. I would see what people really do, and things that really happened -- things that most people would never imagine. People would tell their secrets behind my back as if I wasn't there. I'd hear the various sides of a story that never make it to the nightly news. I got friends from 58 different countries, and got to know different types of people, as well as important variations in culture. All of this exposure to the real world can torture us with realization -- that we live in a world of extraordinary popular delusions. This book series is diverse in scope in every way. There is something for just about everyone to disagree with -- something that may at the same time thrill someone else. It presents just one part of the story, and might be considered an exercise in critical thinking -- the other part of the story requires you to think. Some people won't like my opinions, but they aren't my opinions, they are just what I saw through another window to the real world – and how I survived it in the seat of a taxicab.

Many people told me their complaints about the world, and asked me to tell others. From this forum on wheels we not only tossed around issues, but we also came up with solutions that are hard to tell -- or be heard in a world swept up in a hurricane of noise. I learned people's secrets for 35 years, and decided it's time to tell all. Here it is, and you may want to read it twice -- and buy 5 paperback copies for your friends.

It's like the keys you left on your desk, and you searched to whole office but couldn't find the keys -- when the whole time they were right in front of your face. There is a lot that goes on right in front of us that we don't seem to notice -- this book throws it in your face, and may seem like a bumpy cab ride to a mysterious destination -- but there are things along the way that you can put together like the pieces of a jigsaw puzzle, and depending on how you digest it, get a fresh picture of the world -- a world that needs new direction, because it may appear to be headed for Hell. You are along for the ride whether you like it or not. It's up to you to do something, and this book series may have a story hidden in it somewhere that you really need to know. Take a couple of rides with me, and you may find new doors to adventure and change, and along the way be handed the keys to a new world.

Confessions from a Hell Bound Taxi.

Book I: *Introduction to the Real World*

Her hair edged its way across my face as she pressed her head against my shoulder. Hair spray bristles mixed with the smell of yesterday's toiletry chemicals made me grimace, but I didn't complain even as I got a mouthful of hair. If I was only pretending to be her friend, it was far more real than the many men's fantasies that engaged her life. She wanted to tell me how she hated her life and hated her job, but had trouble finding the words, yet found comfort in talking to me because I represented understanding. A tear fell on my sleeve. She lifted her chest to stick her breasts in my face, and her mood elevated as she became flirtatious with me. She wiped a tear from her eye and looked at me as if she was forming a desperate bond. I was often with her, but someone outside the network of horrors in her life-- she was just a customer.

She grabbed my arm, and said; "Come wit me, dis where da pimp stay."

I had no idea where we were, but being invited into a pimp's house sounded kind of scary. We got out of the taxicab and I followed her with some reluctance. As we approached the door she immediately dropped her charm-- putting on a rather smug look. With a steady rhythm she knocked on the door six times. I waited with her silently for what seemed to be a long time. Finally, the door opened and she took my arm to bring me in with her. Several people came to answer the door, and suddenly we were surrounded by what appeared to be an unsavory lot. A rather large, and good-looking black man was noticeably the boss. A charming gentlemen for about two seconds, then clearly not pleased by seeing me there. I felt in danger as if I had fallen into a pit of snakes.

"He's the cabdriver," she said.

The mood seemed to lift slightly, and fake smiles grew a little wider. Being a taxi driver is like being an ambassador to the underworld. I could be in the company of criminals, and avoid being a victim, or the accused-- depending upon who was taking aim. I wasn't sure these people recognized my 'ambassadorship', and this encounter was just another part of my frightening initiation as the cabdriver.

On any day, at any minute, a cabdriver can be killed. Taxi driving is frequently rated as the one of the most dangerous jobs a person could have. Walking into the pimp's den was part of it, and it didn't look good – some of the people I saw there fit descriptions from recent robberies.

They stood there scrutinizing me for a moment, then the pimp motioned me to go somewhere with one of his homies. With hardly a word, an exquisitely dressed gentleman sporting a peacock tie, and the largest of fake smiles, escorted me to the basement. I pondered my impending demise, and considered my bad judgment as we walked down a narrow flight of stairs-- to a dungeon I might be tortured in, perhaps.

The basement turned out to be a large room with nothing in it at all except for an old jukebox sitting in the middle of the concrete floor. The man with the peacock tie pushed a button -- making gestures as if something exciting was about to happen. Fixed with that sinister smile, and his eyes suspiciously looking down at me-- we stood there together as the music played.

Feeling awkward about the silence, I commented: "That's a good idea-- not to scratch your records that way."

The overdressed gentlemen nodded and stood there with an evermore-sinister looking grin. I felt caught in a mix between boredom and fear as we just stood there, and stood there longer, as yet another song that I didn't want to hear took its turn.

Finally, he said something: "I'm a pimp." I looked at him silently, and after a brief pause his smile grew wider as he informed me yet again, "I'm a pimp".

OK, what was I supposed to say? I nodded, made my own fake smile, and pointed at the jukebox. We stood around, and he let me know a few more times that he was a pimp. I felt like I might as well be having a conversation with a parrot.

Nerves rattled to pieces, I was relieved when the basement door opened and the girls voice called down; "Let's go!" We got out of there quick, and I was glad the detour was over as we drove away from "where da pimp stay." How did I get into this?

I was on the road as an advertising salesman and got into an argument with my boss -- and thought I'd risk danger before putting up with any more crap. Why not try driving a cab in Seattle for a while? I could get to know the place, and take my time finding the right job. I didn't know my way around Seattle at all, but the customers seemed happy to give me directions. I had no idea what I was in for. On my first night a guy who had been stabbed stumbled into my cab. He was bleeding all over the place, and for some reason I believed it was my duty and responsibility to rush him to the hospital.

The dispatcher later explained to me: "It's not your responsibility, you're not an ambulance." But if I had left him to wait for an ambulance he would've bled to death. I drove the guy to the hospital alright, and on the way I had to duck because he was swinging at me trying to sock me in the head while I was driving. So, this is what cab driving is going to be like?! Every day when I went to work I tried to resolve in my mind the dangers of my occupation. I counted the number of taxi cabs compared to the number of drivers killed, and tried to figure the odds of how long I'd survive. I decided to not plan on driving taxicab very long. It was too dangerous, but for at least a moment it was tremendously interesting.

I'd drive aimlessly around the streets of Seattle and see everything that people were doing. I saw people get robbed on the street as if they were asking for it, and I saw police beat people who didn't seem to deserve it. I saw lots of kids running around late at night and wondered what they were doing -- wild things, I imagined. People told secrets in the back of my cab as if I wasn't even there. I knew about everybody's business, and came to realize that a lot of things that we might believe in are not necessarily true. What we believe is biased -- even though we've heard that there are two sides to every story. We ignore that there may be many sides beyond the ones we choose to cling to. Too young to know much, and old enough to think I knew everything... cab driving gave me a real rude awakening. It was an exciting window to the world, a shocking revelation of reality.

In my early twenties I found cruising the red light district to be especially interesting, and I got to know just about every whore in town. A lot of people imagine some thrill or glamour with the ladies that walk the streets at night, and might be surprised to know that they really, really hate sex. Just like other people hate their job, whorin' is rather ugly work sometimes -- but they'll never let you know that.

Their job is to lure men into a trap like a moth to a flame, and get as much as they can out of them while doing as little as possible. But the life of a prostitute has horrible consequences. Once they give in to the lure of easy money, they can easily get trapped into the routine-- their dreams eventually spiraling downward. Life in the sewer awaits. As their sexiness declines, their skill as a pickpocket must improve. There comes a point when there's no way out except straight into the gutter.

Any system of living can trap us once we embrace it, and we turn so much over to automatic thinking, so much, that we might not even notice when we're on an express train to catastrophe. We go along for the ride urging the conductor to go forward, failing to see outside of the trap at all. The lady who worked at Woolworths for 35 years, the guy who worked at the Chevron for 20 years, or the convict doing a life sentence—Did they all plan it that way? Even the lawyer or doctor who initially had some kind of a plan often ended up just falling into an unexpected slot. We should always remember: If you don't plan where you are going you might end up some place you don't want to be.

In this world infected by artifice, and driven by illusion; taxi drivers, prostitutes, hairdressers, waitresses, and bartenders share a unique understanding of the real world. So, the girls out in the night didn't have to play the game with me; I knew the real world too. They could tell me their secrets, and I'd understand. In a lifestyle that can lead to having no real friends, I was the best friend that they had. Reliable transportation can be a big deal when you're desperate-- and the driver, a dear friend.

For me it was a matter of safety and convenience. I could start late and avoid most of the dangerous traffic, and start my shift picking up a bunch of girls to drop off on the 'Ho Stro'. It was a fat fare with a good tip, which insured to them they'd have a quick ride home at the end of the night-- because I had to wait 'till then to get paid.

Other drivers weren't so reliable, and wouldn't give credit even for a few hours. I was treated like a true friend. It was big fun, quite profitable, and seemed to improve my odds for safety. Safety had been a haunting thought. I had imagined so much about how I could get killed driving cab, but didn't have statistics about pimp's basements... among other unknown possibilities that worried me. It appeared that no compromise would guarantee safety in the world of the taxicab. I'll always remember the night when I left the pimp's place, flying to pick up the rest of the girls as if escaping from Hell.

The pimp is perhaps the most despicable part of the prostitution game, but whom can we really blame? The pimps are praised in popular culture, but why? The Ladies of the Night grew to not want any man-- except for the purpose of protection-- and what they might really want most is to protect their dreams. Dreams that would lead to nightmares, but once the dreams begin to fade; by then, so caught up in the routine, they continued, as if the dream still felt real -- even though it had become pathetically absurd. A pimp could use drugs to pump up the dream -- and squeeze every last nickel they could get out of an old whore. It's a disgusting and despicable game.

After dropping off the last of the girls I felt like I wanted to wash my hands, get some coffee-- get out of the cab and away for a minute. From a café window I watched the people milling around Downtown, and wondered if perhaps, like others, I could fall prey to some sordid set of daily rituals, and then; with the terror of the unknown hissing at me, cling to some mundane madness like a familiar friend.

The sight of the meter maid approaching interrupted my daydream. What a disgusting bureaucratic scheme to swindle the public, and all I wanted to do was get a cup of coffee. I ran out to my taxicab just as the government whore with her computerized ticket wizard finished tagging all of the five cars behind my taxi.

"Can I park here?" I asked, as I open the door.

"No," she replied with cold indifference. As she lifted her machine slowly like the blade of a guillotine, the message came through clearly that I'd better get lost. As only a cabdriver can, I was gone before she could push a button. I took the encounter calmly, all in due course, because there was plenty more around to get me angry.

I got in a fistfight about once a week, and hadn't yet learned how to avoid it – but I was certainly trying. One day I saw a handicapped guy-- good, I thought --he'd be safe enough to pick up. I didn't feel like fighting, and he didn't look like a threat. He certainly needed a ride. He was getting around using a pair of crutches, and it looked like both his legs were prosthetics as he lifted his crutch to hail me. I pulled the cab to the curb-- ready to provide the same friendly service that I believed the often-neglected handicapped customer always deserves. I got out of the cab and cheerfully opened the door. I asked the customer where he wanted to go, and if he needed help getting in.

"No thanks," he said, as is often the case with the handicapped. Just because a person has a little disability doesn't mean they want to feel helpless. "I'm slow … takes time," he said.

"Take your time, I'll be patient." The guy struggled for several minutes trying to negotiate his legs into the cab.

All of this time a couple stood across the street with a look of awe, watching, and finally one of them started yelling: "Ass hole, why don't you help him!" A guy ran over, scolding me for being such a rotten cab driver as he crossed the street. "I'll help him, you asshole," he said, as he reached over to put his hand on my customer.

The customer, with one leg in the car, raised his crutch as to defend himself from a potential attacker, and yelled; "Fuck off!"

OK, I'll help him, I thought, and now I was getting in a fistfight to protect my customer. So much for thinking I'd avoid a squabble by picking this guy up.

Things aren't necessarily the way we might assume, and we might be well advised to keep our imagination in check – lest we believe things without recognizing alternatives. As soon as we decide to speculate, we might abandon our quest for perspective, and become fixed in a personal vanity -- of thinking we know something. I was beginning to discover an unbelievable reality, and wondered what we were all thinking. Was anything I thought I knew really true? There are lots of things that really happen, and lots of things that people really do, but even when they happen right in front of our face we sometimes try to deny their very existence. I had to wonder what was real... when confronted by an army of denial. Some people act as if they will turn to stone if they dare to look at some evil thing that we're all supposed to pretend doesn't exist. We even demonize things, so as to make up excuses to not look-- not to allow our fantasies to become tainted by acknowledging reality. We trick ourselves because we operate so much on automatic thinking. A mode of superficiality surrounds us. We are inundated with BS, and by its devices rewire our brains whenever we embrace an engagement, thus transcribing our destiny. It is hard to change ourselves when we aren't even all there. It was a scary thought. I was determined to find out what was really going on. I was learning a lot about people, and still had a lot to learn. I asked people some questions about what was wrong with the picture. It seemed that my personal ambition was to go against the status quo -- I knew I was confused.

For the sake of more practical edification I was learning advanced driving skills.

You don't know how to drive just because you know the rules; you need to practice driving for a few years to fully train your subconscious to do the driving for you, because you don't think about what to do-- how to steer or put on the brake while you're driving. Through practice you train your subconscious to do it automatically.

It takes about 5 years of practice for the average person to really develop driving skill – and then our style doesn't change easily. People think they can do it all along from the beginning, or can change their driving behavior any time – and they learn their mistakes by accident.

Every night of the week, after finishing a 12-hour nonstop driving adventure, I couldn't wait to go back to work the next day. I was getting lots of practice, and learned the hard way with a few crashes. My intense driving practice was highlighted by totaling three taxicabs. In one of the wrecks I'm certain I would have been killed if I had been wearing a seat belt. I never wore seat belts. Taxi drivers were exempt from the rule. Seat belts aren't really necessary, and we should never want them to be. What other illusions might we subscribe to?

My experience in the advertising business got me worried about the seat belt campaign when the law first appeared. I surveyed my customers, and most didn't like the idea of the authorities forcing safety on the public. People didn't care about it that much at first, because you couldn't get a seat belt ticket unless you were stopped for something else, and the fine was minimal. There was a little debate about the necessity of seat belts, and then the advertising campaign grew large, showcasing statistics that seat belts would save lives... with graphic examples to draw our sympathy. I was suspicious of government sneaky tricks as tickets started being issued for seat belt violations alone, and the fines started going up, and there was talk that taxi drivers would be required to wear them soon.

One customer described how he could strangle me with the seat belt, and I didn't even want the things in the cab at all. The general public didn't officially express their distaste of the law, but taxi lobbyists were at work. The enforcers decided to leave the taxi drivers alone, because they determined that the safety issue was different in the taxi circumstance. Statistics about the benefit of seat belts would also be different for different types of cars, for different types of drivers, or for other different circumstances – it doesn't apply universally except for the sake of revenue. The seat belt law did 4 things: 1) It produced revenue – a way of taxing the poor. 2) It conditioned the public to obey. 3) It made money for insurance companies. 4) It made some people safer, sometimes, maybe. Reason can be abandoned when the insurance companies and the government can make money – and the public doesn't protest. The biggest proponent and benefactor of seat belt law was, as a matter of fact, the insurance industry. Your individual difference doesn't matter to a big corporation – to them you're just a number, and if you survive a car crash because you are thrown from a vehicle that is smashed it will cost the insurance companies more money than if you were strapped in and got killed.

Of course the head of the Department of Transportation would also disagree with me, and; to make it look like he is doing his job he will reiterate the commonly advertised beliefs about hands on the wheel making drivers pay better attention, or something. The director will claim that the solution is more enforcement – blind enforcement, as if nobody ever made mistakes that should be forgiven. Every human error is not a negligent act to merit putting a driver in a pillory. If humans don't operate with the predictability of machines – then, should their lives be dismantled? The director thinks so, and will get crazy MADD people to support him.

The director will cite statistics, prepared by law enforcement agencies of course, that declare the effectiveness of law enforcement. Calling for strict enforcement makes it look like he can't be blamed for not doing his job – he'll force everyone to be safe.

We don't need to be terrorized, do we? His job could be eliminated... I think so.

It seems that statistics can be twisted to support any claim, and the public goes along with too much, too easy. I don't appreciate people trying to force me to be safe, because they can't keep me safe. Other people don't necessarily know what I have to deal with when they are standing out of my shoes. The public wants safety, or at least is told that they do-- and get coerced into giving up some of their liberty. The claims don't account for all the variables involved, and imaginary stuff takes precedence over reality. Even the value of police is somewhat an illusion, propped up by unscrupulous politicians, and a sensation hungry media. Police can't solve your personal problems, and in the minds of the public the police are supposed to do things that are even beyond human abilities. In the seat of a taxicab I can't afford the luxury of the fantasies believed by the watchers of silly dramas on TV, or childhood dreams of a superhero cop who flies through the air and always quite ethically gets the bad guys. I could get killed at any minute, and there's no way that the police could protect me. The customer could direct me to an area where there were no police around, by a Kryptonite dumpsite, and pull an axe out from under his coat. Give me the freedom to keep myself safe through my own choice – please! Trouble usually didn't call, and then wait around, so; playing the radio might be safer--it was my choice. Safety must ultimately be a personal responsibility.

The radio had two channels, and one of the channels (by some coincidence) included a number of predominantly black neighborhoods.

Black people couldn't get a cab, not just because they're black (like some people might say), but also because over 90% of all taxicab robberies were committed by African-American males between the age of 15 and 35. Channel 2 was always busy because most drivers chose to avoid the anticipated extra danger, and felt like the customers were harder to serve anyway, often being more demanding. But on a slow night I didn't want to sit around waiting for the little lady from Pasadena to get off the bus. I'm from Oakland, and I could tell real people from bullshit, so I'd keep real busy some nights picking up black people. For all practical purposes, they'd become a skeleton before they got a taxi, but for some reason kept calling, and got lucky that I showed up for them, often surprised I was white... But most black drivers adamantly refused to pick up blacks. The tips were lousy, and I sometimes picked up in neighborhoods where the police wouldn't even go. Somehow I managed to survive, and this made me suspicious. I felt certain that a lot of those people who believe that they are safe because there are police around... would have been safe anyway.

Rules don't necessarily make people behave, and in order to survive I didn't necessarily obey the rules. I'm 100% barbarian and it is discrimination against my cultural orientation to expect me to obey the rules. For sure the police couldn't protect me, and despite all laws against it I was often heavily armed – guns, knives, and at one point I even carried a hand grenade. An errant customer quickly calmed down -- he understood what I was saying even though I couldn't speak clearly with the grenade pin between my teeth. He knew I was crazy, and it was an impression that I felt I had to project in order to do some of the things that I was doing, and still live to tell.

If I was ever scared -- it scares me most that the public doesn't know better, and can't escape what seems to be a whole catalog of ongoing delusions. The public is bombarded by lies on a daily basis to a point of sensory overload.

Whoever knew something was wrong...nobody would fix it later, because those growing up into it wouldn't know any better...we had to act, but just watched it happen. Somebody else would take care of it, we imagine, as we desperately cling to an illusion that everything is OK. Could it be that we might become too distressed in the face of truth, and creep deeper into hiding in the realm of somnambulism? With all of the automation and data overload its hard to think in real time, and with our minds on autopilot we drone through life imagining we are in possession of facts, and capable of reason, simply because we have beliefs. We want to believe, we don't want to think, and appear to be collectively losing our ability to reason at all.

We can look at a mountain of evidence to the contrary and still insist: Handicapped people always want help. Prostitutes really love sex. We need more police. ...etc.

All that I was experiencing was driving me to drink. Was it really? The disturbing things that go on in the world got to bother me, because so much seemed so contrary to what people believe. By the very measure of what I would like to protest -- a popular cognitive construct kicked in: People have things that are too much to deal with, so they drink to escape... find relief... feel better... have fun. As if this worked -- that's why I started drinking -- because of an illusion tossed nonchalantly around the background of the common mind. Drinking didn't escape from anything -- It was more likely to cause problems, and was just something to do, but once I embraced the game it became a habit. Every afternoon before I went to work I drank a large glass or raspberry brandy, alternating with scotch, or gin, or something else.

I got well involved in my study of alcohol, and invented a favorite concoction of Zubrovka with a splash of Tuaca. It was a strong drink, something like a mix called a Rusty Nail, but with Buffalo Grass vodka & Italian liquor instead of Scotch & Drambuie. I referred to it as a Barbarian Sword.

Sometimes I had more than one glass before work, and often staggered into the lot to start my shift. Eventually, I became quite expert at drunk driving. Believe it or not, such a thing can be learned. Most people wouldn't believe the true facts, but they believe a lot of things, and so did I – I believed in teachers, doctors, and other things. Don't we all?

What should we believe? *Seat Belts Save Lives; The Police Keep You Safe*, etc.... just ad slogans. What would doctors have to sell? As a taxi driver in Seattle I didn't have a health care plan, but I got sick-- very sick, and doctors could not identify my affliction. My joints would freeze up, and when I woke up in the morning I couldn't move. I tried to move, and eventually could move slowly, and it took me about 45 minutes to get out of bed. Once I got out of bed, at any moment, I could experience a sensation as if a nail had been driven into my head, and then shot down one side of my body. Half of my body would grow numb, and then I would randomly developed muscle spasms in various locations.

We are supposed to believe in doctors, and I went to them for months-- accumulating a table full of pills, but no progress toward relief. Angry, frustrated, and highly motivated to escape a daily torture, I searched libraries, and talked to countless people.

I decided to try a diet & exercise program that claimed to cure disease. This particular diet and exercise program was difficult to follow, but I was motivated, and it not only worked, but in a few months I was healthier than I think I had ever been.

I quit drinking, not that drinking had anything to do with the problem-- odd as it may seem, I quit drinking when I didn't even want to quit.

I don't know if it was because I was so focused, or; because the special diet had a releasing effect on a grip of alcohol– as proponents claimed. I just forgot to drink any alcohol.

I drank a lot of a superfood combination I invented made from sweet potato and butternut squash. Diet, or exercise, or meditation - I didn't know, but it wasn't doctors. I certainly wasn't going to believe in doctors anymore. During a doctors convention I talked about what I had done, and several doctors agreed, but acknowledged that it was a lot of work, and most people wanted to buy a quick fix-- so the pharmaceutical companies tried to sell it to them. The heath care system has too much focus on treating symptoms. You can't sell the difficult process of healthy living as easily as you can sell a pill.

I was surprised how naïve I'd been once I realized how many things weren't the way they were supposed to be. Like other people, I had believed things because it was what everyone else seemed to agree with. So, along these lines, I had assumed, after observing what other cabdrivers were doing, that taxis were exempt from all traffic laws. Of course I was proven wrong, and it was a good thing that I had also been thinking, with all the risk involved, that I should be done with driving cab-- that I should quit. The State of Washington more-or-less finally thought so too, but it took a year and a half for me to lose my license.

Suddenly, I had to look for another job. I was supposed to take my time to find the right job in the first place, but I got caught up and took too much time-- now my license was suspended for three years.

In the 1970s, Seattle had rather high unemployment, and the city was spread out-- to get any job, a person pretty much needed a car. I'd have trouble getting a job for 3 years? I was screwed. I walked around downtown, and seeing some of the bums; I wondered how far I was away from living in a dumpster and smelling like piss.

I had enough cash to pay the weekly rent in a residential hotel, due the next day. I'd pay in the afternoon, so I could hang onto my life savings as long as possible. I would go out early in the morning looking for a job, because I would be completely broke by the end of the day.

The next day, the *Seattle Morning News* declared that the drought had ended. I didn't understand what that meant, because in Seattle it seemed like-- if it didn't rain in the morning it rained in the afternoon. I was used to the rain, and sometimes would walk in it and hardly notice it was raining. I never knew that there had been a drought, but now it was over. When I went outside it was raining a little harder than usual, so what? Then suddenly the ocean seemed to come down from the sky. I was walking in ankle-deep water in minutes, and then a wind came up and blew my umbrella inside out. I was instantly soaked as if blasted with a fire hose. I wasn't looking for a job in this, and dreaded going back to pay my rent just to sit in my room, wet and broke.

In the distance I saw the lights of the Amtrak train pulling into town. It looked beautiful with a backdrop of lightning crossing the sky. I was drawn to the train station--A place where lots of bums might be staying dry, and perhaps it was my fate to join them. Somehow I made it there just as the train was pulling out of the station, and as if the conductors voice was commanding me, I jumped aboard. The conductor accepted cash that was totally soaked, and sold me a ticket as if it was normal business. It could have been a train to Chicago, or anywhere. I didn't know and didn't care, except for being out of that crazy storm. It turned out I was going to Oakland. Whatever possessions I had left behind were forgotten as easily as dust on a shelf.

Seattle's rain was still dripping off my clothes when I got off the train in Oakland. I love Oakland, but like a lot of people, retain affinity for my hometown, and I wondered if my feelings weren't just another delusion.

I didn't believe anything anymore. But I felt right to be were I was, and imagined maybe I'd get a job in a radio station or something. As I looked through the help wanted section of the Oakland Tribune, I wondered why the State of California would care about what the State of Washington was doing? So… I went to the DMV to ask about my driver's license. They told me that it had expired about a year ago. "I use public transportation now," I said.

The lady looked at me strangely, and replied; "Well, do you want to renew your license? It'll be $50."

My body froze-- except for the hand that pulled a 50-dollar bill out of a secret pocket. Without another word I walked out with a valid California driver's license. Uplifted with another chance-- as if I hadn't had enough taxi adventure already, I wondered what it would be like to drive a taxicab in San Francisco. I left the DMV and went straight to The City.

Halfway across the San Francisco-Oakland Bay Bridge, through a tunnel passing Treasure Island, the architecture of the bridge itself would suddenly become magnificent. Driving through the tunnel, the spectacular view opened up like a dragons mouth ready to devour me. The City was beautiful, and very hilly -- mountainous by some people's standards. Stacked together, with no space between, ornate Victorian architecture rose up the hillsides, often straddled by fabulous gardens. The streets were clean, and the whole place sparkled. A wonderful place to drive around, I imagined.

In the late 1970s in San Francisco the money was easy, and the rent was cheap. Artists, intellectuals, and other people pursuing some heartfelt interest had mobbed The City. Nobody was forced to chase a buck, and the whole place was a big party that ran 24/7.

Everything would change of course, and I feel sorry for the people who had to miss the wild times. I wasn't going to miss it for anything.

If putting my head in the mouth of an angry shark was safer than driving a cab at night, so what? I was determined to drive a cab in San Francisco. The times were too good.

The City was permeated with an atmosphere of liberty. It seemed that anyone could do anything they wanted, and nobody would care—as long as you don't call it 'Frisco'. Locals, who preferred to call it 'The City', would aggressively reprimand people who dared say 'Frisco'. Outside of the hostility that could arise out of name calling, the people seemed to be outrageously friendly. Everything appeared to be running perfectly -- seemingly untainted by overbearing authorities. Visitors who came to San Francisco were astounded, and I was intent on being more than just a visitor myself. I never wanted to leave, even to go back across the bridge to Oakland. I insisted to myself that it had to be easier to make it here than in Seattle. In my opinion it was mandatory, and I had a license, so...

I went to Yellow Cab and found a crowd of people who were also looking for a job. I ended up going to several companies, and found out it wasn't going to be easy, so I got as much information as I could from other prospective drivers. After failed attempts at a half-dozen companies I applied at what looked like the worst cab company in town, and was rejected there, too. Thoughts of skid row invaded my daydreams. There were certain streets that were like that -- full of drunken bums. Would a dreary fate follow me from Seattle?

Skid row is a term that actually originated in Seattle. It was a nickname for a street where they had once slid logs down a hill to a lumber mill at the docks. It became a street on the edge of town where washed up seamen would congregate, and drink. As the shipping industry declined, the entire waterfront became full of bums. In later years, huge layoffs at Boeing made half of downtown look like skid row.

A central spot became Pike Place Market, the place where Starbucks started its business, selling overpriced coffee to tourists who were loose with their money. A lot of beggars would hang around figuring on spare change in such a scenario. I remembered the fear I had of heading for a life of living in a dumpster, and hanging around Starbucks. I dreaded that there might ever be a Starbucks in San Francisco someday.

When I impulsively jumped on a train in Seattle it seemed to put me on an angels wing, but it wasn't landing me on a job. I wasn't about to just forget about it – I had to find a job. There were several companies in San Francisco, and I visited almost every one after numerous trips to the DMV to get originals of my driving record. There were a couple of cab companies -- so I was told by the mob of applicants at other places -- that required experience, and had long waiting lists for available openings. I was running out of places to go – I had to make a plan, and a plan requires a goal, so I had to pick a target. I thought I'd check out this place that was said to be not only the best cab company to work at in San Francisco, but one of the best in the world. Curious about what kind of glorious place this could be, I walked into the DeSoto Cab Company garage to take a look.

It was a far cry from the muddy lot back in Seattle-- where I used to stumble across ruts and potholes, and then wait for maybe an hour in the rain to take out a wreck to ride in. In Seattle an ornery old man would give out the cabs, and if I complained that the one he was giving me was dented too much, and stinks, and shimmies, or whatever; he'd reply: "What do you want, a gold-plated Cadillac? The meter works, and the car pushes easy, so get the hell out of here!"

No, this place in SF had brand-new cars that looked like they all had just been waxed. I walked around the busy garage and got directions to the manager's office. Everyone seemed to be friendly, very happy.

I heard the dispatch radio, and the voice sounded like an auctioneer giving out calls in rapid succession. This was taxi heaven. I was elated that there was such a treasure, but intimidated by the fact that I couldn't have it.

I approached the manager's door, and on it there was a large sign -- *Not Hiring*. I had to find out what it would take, so I could plan for the future, and I knocked on the door -- braced for rejection. A friendly gentleman answered, and identified himself as the manager.

"I noticed your sign," I said, "but I just wanted to know..."

The manager interrupted me; "That's not for you. Come on in."

The hardest place to get hired turned out to be the easiest place for me to get an interview. I walked out of the place stunned that I'd just been hired. Back then they not only had new cars, and lots of business, but there were benefits: medical and dental, paid vacation, retirement, and a lot of things that you'd never even expect from a job that offered so much independence. Most cab companies didn't have this, and years later these benefits would no longer exist anywhere (eliminated under the guise of doing taxi drivers a favor), but no benefit could compare to the freedom and adventure in driving a cab — if you were brave enough to venture it.

Driving cab in San Francisco was like going to a billionaire's cocktail party. Like milling around at a huge party meeting the rich and famous. Of course there'd be a little riffraff in the mix, and a lot of servants. There was a big service economy in San Francisco that catered to people who came from around the world for meetings.

The service workers were extraordinary, and even treated the riffraff like kings — quite appropriately, not judging. A person with the appearance of riffraff could be a savant genius, a great artist, or a celebrity in disguise.

Celebrities would come for a vacation. Business people would come to do business. Crazy people could come to escape their craziness in a city where a person could do whatever they wanted, and have the most outrageous peculiarities ignored. Everyone seemed to be coming to San Francisco, imbuing it with tremendous diversity. A spirit of love and acceptance floated in the air as much as the fog that often covered The City. This was truly a wonderful place, and the job of dreams was in my hands– to drive a taxi --to cruise around the beautiful hills, and interact with all sorts of people and surprises, either wonderful or weird. It was a fabulous adventure. There didn't seem to be any rules to take precedence over just having a ball. San Francisco was a paradise in the '70s.

Compared with Seattle this was a whole new taxi adventure. A different flavor, and more candy. I didn't have to try hard, and could waste a lot of time fooling around and still make a living. I made up an excuse – that I needed to get a better grasp of what was happening on the streets -- to justify fooling around a lot.

The *ladies of the night* had been a mainstay of my business in Seattle, and I was looking, but it was different here. There were high-priced hookers on Powell Street, and fitting the atmosphere of freedom, there were no pimps. These women never took a cab, and some of them drove Porsches. Down near the end of the cable car line, right on Ellis Street, and up a few blocks there were a variety of street walkers that were more familiar to me--forced into prostitution for the sake of drugs. Powell Street prostitutes might be legal secretaries by day, women who normally wouldn't engage in prostitution, but were interested in a bit of the big money as a sideline. If a gal got caught up on drugs, she could end up around corner in the bargain basement known as the Tenderloin.

The whole Tenderloin section of San Francisco — west of Powell and south of Geary--had been known for prostitution from earlier days when the city was a busy seaport.

Now these streets, lined with rundown residential hotels, had become a place for drugs, cheap whores, and anything goes. Fancy restaurants and theaters that had been long established continued to do business even though the neighborhood had become a bit unsavory for an evening stroll. Quite often, people wanted to get out of the area – and of course there were people who wanted to go there only for the sake of evil deeds. I had an attraction to cruising streets where people might be desperate for a cab. I also liked to flirt with the dangers of the neighborhood rather than be afraid. I patrolled the more sordid streets as if a warrior surveying a battlefield.

Of course I didn't spend all of my time cruising the Tenderloin – I spent a lot of time at Fisherman's Wharf, or driving through Golden Gate Park, or through the many beautiful neighborhoods around *The City*. The neighborhoods still had distinct characteristics, and within a few blocks a neighborhood could completely change to something else. One world would fade into another, and it made The City very interesting.

Specific neighborhoods really meant something in those days. People in the 1970s seemed to congregate in neighborhoods that fit their character, and the Tenderloin was like the dump for impoverished characters, and outcasts. Society operated like a remnant from the days before the Fair Housing Act when people actually could control their own neighborhoods. People who had lived someplace for a while would still try to hang on to the family-like feel about their neighborhood, and actually continued to talk to some of their neighbors. In contrast, the Tenderloin was out of control, absent of family, and you'd better not even talk to people you didn't know.

Downtown, the neighborhoods seemed to improve dramatically as you went further up the hill (as did snobbery).

The highpoint of luxury was the Top of Nob Hill, and rumor has it that the name originated out of common use — what people called it — with the 's' left off of 'snob' as a mockery.

The Tenderloin was at the bottom — a place for laborers, misfits, elderly with inadequate pensions, parolees, young people just getting on their feet, or the bankrupt (who could sometimes tell tales about how awful their old neighbors up the hill had been).

In other parts of town the position on the hill didn't mean so much, but sometimes people had an attitude about their territory. The top of Twin Peaks was expensive, but on the bottom of the hill on the other side was the exclusive St Francis Woods. I didn't know if I could live there, or if I'd want to. Willie Mays couldn't buy a house in St. Francis Woods, because of a race discrimination clause connected with a house. Was it just that house, or all houses in St. Francis Woods? It might have been all to get publicity, or to make an issue. After mixing race with real estate was outlawed, African-Americans still were not choosing to live in St. Francis Woods. Would Willie Mays have contributed anything to the neighborhood? Would the neighborhood contribute anything to him? I don't necessarily understand these issues, because; suppose there's a square dance going on out in the country, a real big wing-ding, and no African-Americans will be there... would they want to, or is someone keeping them out? I didn't know the answer, and wondered how much trouble I would have moving into a black neighborhood--even though it was allowed by law.

In any well-integrated neighborhood anyone might have to gain acceptance regardless of race, but color drew special lines -- often reflected by price.

Most of The City had bargain residences scattered between some of the most luxurious neighborhoods in the world. I often imagined where I might rent.

I could enjoy cheap rent in a black neighborhood-- with a view of mansions, I thought, but I was scared to make the move. I certainly wasn't going to afford to live in a mansion by driving a cab, and it didn't matter, because I practically lived in the cab.

My life was totally consumed by the taxi. I'd wait around the garage for a couple of hours sometimes, and then drive for up to 12 hours every day. The cab took all my time -- if I slept on a park bench it wouldn't make much difference. I would never live in St. Francis Woods... I'd park at St. Francis hotel, maybe.

To begin my shift I often headed toward the St. Francis Hotel on Powell Street at Union Square. Taxicabs would line up in front of the St. Francis Hotel, but I wouldn't stop unless the line was almost empty – or on a slow night when there was nothing else to do. Usually, I cruised continuously all night, only stopping to pick up or drop off a customer. At any time I could catch a ride that could end me up anywhere. If I didn't find a fare I often followed routes that I'd invent to give myself some kind of direction. I could go down Powell Street past the St Francis, make a right on Ellis, then maybe hook around and go back by Union Square and into Chinatown. Or I might head down to Market Street, up Van Ness, along the Fisherman's Wharf, then down the Embarcadero – making a big circle. I'd hope to never complete such a big circle without getting a fare, but often did on a slow Monday night.

It was a Tuesday, and after a wearily unprofitable Monday there is often nervous anticipation that Tuesday won't be any better. I left the garage quickly, as if to race the other drivers for a spot in line at the St. Francis.

I wondered what the night would be like, and if the hotel line would be full, but just two blocks from the garage my spirits were lifted when I spotting a fare on the corner.

It was a pair of Japanese tourists, wanting to go to Union Square to take pictures. It was a short ride, but it was great to get paid to go to where I was going anyway -- I could pull in to the back of the cab line at the St. Francis, and drop them off there. I wasn't going to be so lucky, because I noticed that the cab line was full as we approached the St. Francis -- they really wanted to go across the street to Union Square Park anyway, and at least I got a small fare to start the shift. As the Japanese tourists were getting out of the cab, a couple of well-dressed gentlemen came out of the park to take over the cab as it was being vacated -- so, you never know where luck will find you. It's best to keep a positive attitude lest you chase the luck away. The gentlemen wanted to make a couple of stops. "Don't worry, we'll tip you," they said. It looked like it was going to be a good ride as they directed me around to do whatever they were doing. Their conversation was vague, and I became curious.

"What kind of business are you in?" I asked, during a pause in their talk about nothing.

"Spice," said one of them, as he gave me a look of impatience – "We're in the spice business."

"Oh… a lot of exotic spices are becoming popular these days, aren't they? What's your favorite spice?" I asked, feeling awkward about talking out of place.

"Pepper, my favorite spice is pepper," he said.

The tone was as if to throw the pepper in my face. Whatever his business -- was none of my business. It was time to shut up. I continued the ride without any more comment, and ended up dropping them off at a high-priced view condo -- so high over the city that you'd only see fog. They paid with a substantial tip.

As my customers were getting out of the cab I noticed a beautiful red-haired woman standing in the street. She was waiting for a cab that wasn't showing up.

I backed out into the street, and she lifted her arm. I hollered at her; "Driving around up here in the clouds, I should be so lucky to be saluted by an angel."

"Can I get a cab?" she said, laughing, "I need to get to Macy's."

"Of course -- this is my lucky night," I said. I certainly felt lucky, topping off three fares in a row with one of the most beautiful red-haired women I'd ever seen. She got in, and as we were driving down Twin Peaks through the fog I was glad to have a long ride -- not for the money, but for a better chance to start conversation. I said nothing for a little while, wanting to be cautious, until halfway down the hill while still in a blinding fog I commented; "Nice view."

"Oh yes," she said, jokingly, "people pay a lot of money for this."

Having progressed so far with a little humor, I took the liberty to get a little more personal; "You have red hair. Is that natural hair color?"

"It is," she answered.

"Did you know that Thomas Jefferson had red hair?" I asked.

"I did," she said, "and George Washington also had red hair when he was young, but it turned white -- it's genetic."

Evidently, I had starting something more than I wanted to, as she went on about the genetics of red-haired people all the way downtown. She seemed concerned, that; at the rate that fewer red-haired people were being born -- in 40 years no more red-haired people would be born at all. Is it possible that people like George Washington and Thomas Jefferson could be considered an endangered species? She went on, and before I was compelled to agree or disagree I was dropping her off.

I had been on a roll, and ended up back around Union Square. The hotel lines looked full, and I saw plenty of empty cabs driving around hoping for the same kind of luck I'd had ...it wasn't a busy night.

To avoid the competition, and perhaps keep my roll going, I headed down Ellis -- thinking of less desirable pickings in the Tenderloin. I made a left on Hyde, and then left again on Eddy, following the one-way streets. Weaving down the hill I was cruising deeper into the sleaze. I passed a small crowd doing some kind of drug deals, and then saw a guy down the block waving his arms. He didn't look too scruffy, and didn't look hopped up. He might have just scored, but he looked more like a square, blue-collar guy, who had been looking for a cheap whore, and wandered into the wrong area. He didn't look like he belonged down here -- sort of clean cut, in his late twenties, and I didn't believe him to be a threat. I steered the cab in his direction as if to run him over. If he had an attitude I could evaluate his reaction, and determine how much trouble he might be before we went anywhere. He jumped into the cab as if the threat of becoming road kill hadn't fazed him. He just seemed happy to get a ride.

"So, where do you want to go?" I asked.

"Where the girls are," he said.

"What do you mean, like a strip club?"

"No, a cheap one on the street that I can take back to my room. Just drive around."

Sure enough, he just wanted to ride around and look for a girl.

"OK, but I can't give you any advice. I'll just drive, and you tell me when to turn." I drove aimlessly around the Tenderloin while the guy made comments about sleazy whores, and still wanted to look at more.

I wasn't having fun with him. He became uncomfortable, and tried to salvage his mood, awkwardly.

"Anyone ever run?" he asked; "I imagine it happens all the time."

I snapped at him; "Is that what you think? Is that what you did when you were younger?"

"No, man, come on," he pleaded.

"Well, people don't run," I told him.

"But they might try to rob you," he said.

"No way, I don't pick of people who want to rob me."

"How can you tell?" he asked.

I replied; "I can tell you're an asshole".... and after a pause, told him, "Just kidding." I was losing interest in listening to this guy, and overran the conversation with more of an explanation than he asked for: "By the way people talk I might tell what kind of work they do. I can tell if a person is Filipino, Chinese, or Korean -- and a lot of people think all Far East Asians are the same, but they're quit different from one another. Vietnamese people can drive. Chinese people like rules too much, and there are no spelled out specific instructions on how you steer a car to make a left turn."

I suppose the guy interpreted my comments as having to do with race, and he asked the question: "Do you ever pick of black people?"

I responded, forcefully, as if to shut him up; "Hey, I even pick up Irish people. They want to fight each other, or me, at any time."

"Irish were discriminated against, didn't they…?"

"Didn't I pick up an asshole?" I said, "Don't confuse yourself with *magic words*."

"What magic words? Lucky charms?"

"Just one word — that word — and, yes, they were discriminated against for decades in America, and contributed much more than has ever been credited. The Irish faced discrimination in odd ways sometimes -- like a lot of people. Once I met a Chinese guy who described to me how he felt the pain of racism. He had just met an Irishman. He interpreted a confrontational manner as being racist, but a lot of Irish people cling to a culture of Individualism, and to be confrontational is just a characteristic of the culture — so in a sense the Chinese guys interpretation of racism might in itself be considered racist."

"Yeah, I guess...," he acknowledged, "there are a lot of different cultures, and we can't expect other people to think like us – in China, Confucius got some sayings I don't need to hear." "You've got to believe in God," he said; "and I'm Catholic."

"You're free to choose any religion you want – supposedly."

"Freedom has a price you know, and we need more military power," he said.

"Oh, bullshit, fighting some imaginary enemy isn't making us free," I said; "we've talked race, religion, and politics, and driven around long enough looking for a tramp to give you a better price, and perhaps give you herpes if you're not careful; and I'm sure you're going to confess to your Priest for what you do"..."America didn't become free because we believed just anything." I was already irritated with the guy, and just as an argument was about to boil over, I glanced over my shoulder to see that he was playing with himself. Our conversation was over. I turned completely around, reached over the back seat, and punched him in the face. "The only war that I care about will be between me and you if you don't get lost," I told him, as he struggled to zip up his pants. I jumped out and opened the door. He came out of the cab swinging. I casually dealt with him as if I was just helping a customer out of the cab as usual. I ducked his blow. He tried to kick me and I slammed the door against him, and then poked him in the eye with my finger. He screamed in a way that the people down the street probably thought some mad woman just lost her crack pipe.

I wondered what the police would say. He wasn't doing anything to me - he was doing it to himself. He hadn't really attacked me, or did he?

He took a swing at me, but it was only after I punched him in the face twice. I didn't know if I could get into trouble for poking him in the eye – I was defending myself from what?

I was a little on edge because of the dangers in the job, and wasn't adding to favorable odds by picking up a guy in a bad neighborhood. Perhaps a fight was understandable. I was yet to become an expert at negotiation, so I still got in too many fights. If I had been a cowardly cop I would've killed several people by now – even for indecent exposure, maybe. That's another hazard I had to watch out for -- the police.

I'd seen things happen, and heard the stories that the nightly news doesn't tell. Police often used deadly force, and claim a threat—but it's more like a far-fetched fantasy than a real threat. They attack citizens because they think an individual made a mistake, but the police make mistakes too. They shouldn't be allowed to shoot anybody. They certainly shouldn't be praised, and rewarded with a paid vacation when they kill citizens at their own convenience. Driving a taxicab is far more dangerous than police work, but I couldn't shoot people if I didn't like dealing with them. I had to learn how to differentiate between real or imagined threats, and I was getting good at it. Police should have even more skill— you'd think. But I had witnessed absurdly inappropriate behavior, and far too much brutality by police. My fighting wasn't so horrible. The guy would survive the poke in the eye. I was becoming fearless about my job as a taxi driver, yet I was worried about the police -- often unreasonable with people. I saw them do crazy things to other people. Maybe I could get in some kind of special trouble for punching a masturbator in the face? I decided it was time to take a break. There were a number of businesses where I had made friends with the owners. I could stop by and use the bathroom, get some coffee, and stand awhile to take a break from sitting down for hours.

There was a corner grocery store in the heart of the tenderloin owned and run by an elderly Chinese man. He would often say that he didn't work for a living -- it was a fight for a living. Of course I could relate to his job description.

He had put his kids through college with his hard labor, but no family or friends dared to help him at the store. He ran the business, and bore the threat of the neighborhood all by himself. He was always happy to see me stop by when I wanted to take a break for a few minutes. It was a break for him to have somebody around that wasn't going to be a problem. Mr. Wong often tried to teach me a few Chinese words while I had a cup of coffee in his store. Deranged people sometimes came in the store to engage Mr. Wong in silly disputes. I'd start trying to talk to the problem person in Chinese. Of course they didn't know what I was talking about. The peculiarity of a white guy speaking Chinese seemed to stun them, and Mr. Wong and I would make a joke of it.

This time when I pulled up at Mr. Wong's grocery store, a couple of teenagers were standing in front. I'd seen these guys around before. As I walked into the store, the larger one asked me; "Excuse me, Mr. Taxi Driver, if we give you $10 could you drive us around for awhile?"

"Well, I have been known to give people rides?" I said.

"You'll do it?" he asked with enthusiasm; "For how long?"

"Oh, maybe a half an hour, but I'm going inside to take a break right now," I said. I didn't want to question his wishes, but the young man's requests seemed a little weird -- and I didn't feel like being a getaway car at the moment, so I quickly excused myself and went into the store. I could hear the taxi radio from inside the store, and it wasn't encouraging. After about five minutes of joking around with Mr. Wong I decided it was time to leave. There didn't seem to be much going on, so...

"Let's have the 10 bucks," I said, as I walked out of the store towards the cab. The boys acted as if they had won something, and quickly held out a $10 bill as they jumped into the back seat. "Well, Where do you want to go?" I asked.

"We don't care, we just want to get off the street for a minute. The cops are assholes."

"OK, I can understand that, but where do you want to go?"

"Anywhere, we don't care... just around the Tenderloin."

"Alright I'll drive around aimlessly, and in a half-hour I'll kick you out wherever we are at the time – Is that what you have in mind?"

"That's OK...you're bein' real cool to do this Mr. Taxi Driver," said the guy who was usually quiet. The one who did all of the talking, introduced himself; "I'm Rubin." Rubin acted overly polite, except that he told me his friends name was 'Creepy'.

They seemed awfully happy to just ride around the Tenderloin, but in a moment they were smoking pot. So that's it. I didn't want any part of it, but I didn't care, shouldn't judge, and wasn't involved in what other people do. As a taxi driver you really can't dictate what your customers should do very much, and it is often best to mind your own business — just collect the fares. Even still, I punched a guy in the face for jacking off, and; for this customer I thought I'd mention: "You know that smoking too much pot can wreck your memory? And if you don't have anything to do it can get in the way of your motivation, and you just sit around and do nothing".

They were laughing.

"Where do you live?" I asked.

One of them answered; "I forgot." Their laughter increased.

"Do either of you have a job?"

Rubin answered by telling an elaborate story about all the pointless things that he did to waste away his day everyday. It seemed like a rather creative parody about my warnings against too much weed.

Rubin seemed to be quite intelligent, rather clever, and outrageously polite. I pointed out that he seemed awfully polite, and he proceeded with another creative story about how he'd been to Charm School.

The two young men were rather amusing, and maybe just wanted a place where they could smoke pot without being bothered. By the time I dropped them off I felt like I had more fun than they did—without the need of smoke. So, what did the pot do? Did they need it? Why should I care? I don't know everything, and teenagers have to figure things out on their own, anyway. Believing that they can be forced to agree seems to be a silly illusion—Teenagers know everything already.

A couple days later I stopped for a flag, but decided I didn't want to give the guy a ride after all. He began flailing a beer can and splattering beer all over my cab, screaming, and spitting at me. Rubin just happened to be across the street at the time, and seeing this, ran over and slammed the guy against the wall. Rubin proceeded to give the assailant a detailed lecture as if he was addressing an audience at a university. The formal speech was rather humorous in the way it was being addressed to a madman. After being slammed against the wall he pausing to listen for a while, but the bum finally recovered enough to complain about the lecture, and then grew hostile again. Rubin abruptly dropped his polite, calm, respectable demeanor, and roared in the guys face like a lion. The tone of his voice, and his fierce look was enough to immediately back the guy off. Without another word the tramp ran away.

"Come on Rubin, let's go," I said, as I got back into the cab. "We'll drive around the block a couple times." Rubin climbed into the front seat.

Rubin, although very intelligent, quite charming, and with the ability to act very respectable—was clearly a street-wise thug. Having a thug on my side might be a good idea.

The acquaintance turned out to be especially rewarding, I thought, when we turned a corner and he asked me to stop -- to introduced me to a girl he saw walking down the street. A couple blocks later we saw another girl, and again we stopped and he introduced me to her. Then we stopped at a small crowd of people. I saw the way he talked to them, and came to the conclusion that Rubin was in a dominant position in the pecking order of kids on the street. He also seemed to know a lot of girls that I hadn't noticed before, and introduced me to about a dozen of them in about as many minutes. In the days that followed, in the course of cruising around town, I'd pick up girls that Rubin had introduced me to. They'd like to take a short ride around the neighborhood with me anytime, and it was like a break for me while still at work -- If I saw a fare I wanted to pick up, the girl would jump out. If there was somebody I didn't want pick up I could say that I had someone already. The law says that I had to pick up anybody that wants a ride, but there were some people I'd be crazy to pick up. I had become somewhat desensitized by danger, and liked to imagine myself fearless – not stupid -- and would get fatigued from having to sort it out. Sometimes I just wanted to pick up one of the girls. The short break seemed good for both of us, and we could share news about what was going on around the block -- real news that might be useful for our survival. Knowledge dissipates fear, but the establishment media wants us to be afraid – their news is no good. Contrary to what the 6 o'clock news would like to let you know -- I realized that most murders were not committed as random acts, but by acquaintances. I just had to be careful about who I got to know. Security was a good enough excuse to ride around with a young girl for a minute, but any excuse to get to know a pretty girl might do. Eventually, I knew quite a few young girls around the streets — invisible to me before I entered Rubin's network. They all were underage prostitutes. Usually they didn't hang on the street very long, and if I ever had seen any of them before, I didn't realize that they were prostitutes. Some of them were as young as 12 years old, and I had never even imagined something like that.

I got to be known on the streets as the cool cab driver, as well as someone not to be messed with. Sometimes the kids would come to me with issues, because I was someone they could talk to in a context where no role positioning had to be maintained. I told a couple people how to solve ridiculously simple problems, and they acted like it was a big deal, as if nobody ever talked to them at all. This might have been part of some attempt at manipulation, I wondered. I wasn't in the business of giving advice, anyway, so it didn't really matter. Then one day when I stopped at a bar to pick someone up -- I got out of the cab, and there was a boy standing on the corner who approached me and asked if he could talk to me for a minute.

"No, I'm busy right now." I said, and walked into the bar to announce that the taxi had arrived. As I was pulling away with the customer, I saw the boy on the corner -- he had a strange look on his face. I think his name was Doug, but I didn't know him.

Later that evening one of the young girls around the block waved me down. I pulled over and she came to the taxi window.

"Hey, you know Doug?" She asked.

"No, not really."

"Well," she said, "he just commit suicide about an hour ago."

Yeah, his name was Doug, and now I should wonder what he wanted to talk to me about. I felt uncomfortable for the rest of the evening, and drove around thinking hard about how it shouldn't be so difficult to talk to people. The things that were going on that shouldn't be going on, and I was looking at it from in the middle of it. I knew too much. Perhaps I should even do more than just talk.

The Tenderloin was a nasty place. I knew it too well, not just because I surveyed its streets every night, but I also lived there.

For about the price of an apartment downtown I could get a rather large flat in a predominantly African-American section of Haight Street, in an area that was known at the time as the Fillmore. For a white guy to move into an all-black neighborhood was as problematic as a black guy moving into an all-white neighborhood. People don't think of it that way, but that's the way it was. There were risks involved in moving into an area where you didn't belong. It didn't bother me so much, the Tenderloin sucked, and I figured I should be able to move into the Fillmore. I didn't think I should have a problem getting along with black people.

Before I moved to Seattle I had lived in Oakland right down the street from Huey Newton. To me he was a champion for rights, and that he focused on black people didn't color my opinion of him as an individual — I admired him, as did a lot of local people. Huey Newton, not Martin Luther King, was the civil rights hero of this Fillmore neighborhood. Who picked Martin Luther King, anyway? Some people would call me a racist if I talked this way – but what race am I, and how does it apply? They act as if something is my fault, and then blame white people for something – what white people are they talking about? There are 7 difference white races, and none of that has much to do with me. Shouldn't we be thinking about individuals instead of race, anyway? These questions came to mind as I considered moving into an all black neighborhood, and thought some of the issues to be strange. Some people even suspected a conspiracy, but I didn't think so -- odd policies were not purposeful as much as they were just a reaction to a sequence of events.

Things can appear to be conspiracies because one event logically leads to another; and there are opportunistic moments when people add input--usually out of fear or greed.

There very well may have been some hidden political conspiracies involving money and power, but there was no conspiracy of races against each other. Something appeared to be going on against the people, and race was just used as an excuse.

I've been accused of being racist against all sorts – from black folks to pit bulls. I think pit bulls are bad dogs – too unpredictable, and capable of harm. I don't like black people that try to rob me, or are pushy and demanding. These opinions are not an issue of race -- if you think about it. I would never agree with what I've heard about abusive segregation in the South, and in no way would want to discount the benefits of civil rights to anyone – but the facts are often presented out of context, with important details missing. The questions are: How much should I believe what I've been told? How can I address people emotionally attached to fallacious reasoning? What should I have to say about things far out of my reach? I was suspicious.

There was something wrong altogether about the focus on race. What was the media doing when it took what should be general complaints, and shifted them to race issues? Even to have discussions about conflict can support the idea of conflict. Is the intent to bring people together, or create conflict – so that, perhaps, we don't recognize the real enemy? Efforts to bring people together are admirable, but the concept is waylaid against kind reasoning if we end up trying to corral people together under a single banner – the whole society could end up becoming like a big prison. What we really should want to do is appreciate people's differences, engage effective communication, and establish appropriate boundaries when necessary. Race talk won't allow any of that. Whatever the issue, when presented as if it's all about race, you can be sure that it's bullshit. It's all about communication.

One day, while walking by Buena Vista Park with a group of people from Berkeley, I saw on opportunity. There was a group of black men sitting in the Park, and on cue to the bleeding heart liberal stereotype applied to Berkeley people, I suggested; "Let's go hang out with them." They couldn't refuse, or they could be accused... So, we walked up the grassy knoll to greet the black folk. The UC Berkeley students sat on the grass as I began to address the black men.

"Hey, I've got an idea," I said, "and I wanted to get your opinion. I want to start a chapter of the Black Knights of the KKK..."

Upon hearing so much of my introduction, the Berkeley crowd jumped up and ran like cheetahs. Seven black men remained sitting on the lawn, drinking, and waiting to see what would happen next. I repeated my initial statement, and continued...

"Just to show that the media driven government is full of bullshit... There aren't bunches of white people trying to lynch blacks, and there isn't all this hate going on. The government is promoting all the hate -- to create problems only they can solve. They are the haters, and all the KKK talk is a bunch of bullshit."

"Yep," said one of the black men.

"Black and white aren't at war," I continued; "the government is the enemy. The police are the haters. People can work it out on their own. The Black Knights can throw a spotlight on the bullshit."

As a finished my speech, the Berkeley group was watching at a distance -- sure that I would be torn to shreds.

"Damn, that's a good idea," said one of the black men.

"Your friends didn't think so," said another.

"They aren't my friends – they'd turn against us all, because they're even afraid to talk. They'll turn against themselves out of ignorance. The Black Knights can save them."

Two of the black men started laughing.

The consensus was that if I set the thing up that they'd all go for it.

We really need to communicate, and there was clearly some confusion. The problem is that we don't look beyond the surface – stuck on the superficial reality of appearances and possessions, which ignore the matter of how people really are. I wanted cheap rent, and I could communicate. Unfortunately, it scared some people – but I was moving in.

Back in the day, an apartment in a black neighborhood was often less than half the price of other neighborhoods. They weren't necessarily bad neighborhoods; you just had to know how to get along. I figured I could handle it, and was excited about getting a huge apartment flat on Haight Street.

When I moved in I didn't exactly expect Welcome Wagon, and I also didn't expect to get robbed right away, but I got burglarized the day after I moved there. The thrill of moving away from the Tenderloin dropped to despair. I stood outside the broken window leading into my apartment, staring at it. I hadn't experienced burglary before, and hadn't given any thought to that type of crime. Not really knowing what to do, I did what a lot of people think they're supposed to do -- I called the police. Here I was, in a new neighborhood where people just might think I didn't belong, and I was sinking into an especially horrible uneasiness. I had heard that the next block up the street had once been rated as having the highest murder rate for any single block in the State. I don't know whose statistics, but any such claim didn't make me feel at all comfortable. When out of a familiar environment I wasn't so fearless as I might have imagined. I called the police from a pay phone, and stood outside the broken window for over two hours waiting for a squad car to arrive. I expected the officer to enter the apartment and make sure it was safe for me to go in.

When I made the suggestion to the officer, he said; "No way, I'm not going in there... "It's your place, you go inside"… "Go ahead, I'm not going to wait around here all day."

He was rude; I was disgusted. I crawled in the window and discovered nobody inside, and it appeared that the only thing that had been stolen was a cheap radio.

I returned to report to the officer, and he told me; "Well, make sure you board up the windows so nobody else can get in." Then he left.

I scratched my head, and thought; I knew all that.

What do we need the police for? Some people claimed that black neighborhoods were deprived of needed police services. Police didn't come, and shouldn't if they weren't called. Black folks just knew better, and didn't call for the police very much.

Police can't solve all of the problems that we can't deal with ourselves. Police themselves can become the problem. Trying to give our problems to the police is silly, and could be just asking for more trouble. We expect police to address all sorts of issues that are far beyond the range of human potential. No wonder police are crazy sometimes. We ask too much. If we ask for more police to stop crime, they'll do that all right – they'll get you if you have an unlicensed dog, or if you forget to put on your seat belt. The public has been brainwashed into thinking that if the police weren't there that nobody in the community would be safe – but the police aren't there! When you call them, even if you only have to wait a few minutes, you could be dead. I know quite well from the taxi experience that they can't keep anyone safe. To handle many of the personal problems that people often call the police for – the police are often practically useless. I had to be responsible for my own safety.

I had a well-hidden shotgun that I dug out, and walked around the neighborhood with it for about an hour to see if I could find some boards lying around to put over my window, so I could sleep comfortably for the night.

The next day I walked out of my apartment, and looked both ways down the block with a feeling like an enemy might be surrounding me. I hoped that they had seen me during my evening stroll with the shotgun. I could've got in a lot of trouble, because Americans hadn't had the right to bear arms since 1968 — I didn't know the rights had been lost, but at least I didn't get caught.

As I stood outside my apartment, irritation gave way to admiration as I looked at the antique architecture that lined the streets for blocks -- tall Victorians as far as I could see. Intricate details that were often hand carved -- highlighted by multi-colored paint. They were very old buildings alive with history, calling out to me to tell me their stories.

Some people might only see the maintenance problems, and not appreciate the artistry and quality of craftsmanship from a century ago. The neighborhood was rundown and dangerous, and perhaps a mistake for me to be there, but as I looked down the street, wondering; I was swept away by the view, admiring the old Victorians that refused to fall down, and caught in a daydream about their history.

Someone started hollering. I turned to look. A woman was coming toward me with a baseball bat in her hand. She came from about three houses down -- from the other side of the street. As she came closer she was still hollering, but I considered that this might be just the way she talks — or was she about to beat me to death? I sat calmly. She wasn't holding the bat as if she was going to swing it at me. Oh, this was the neighborhood equivalent of 'Welcome Wagon', I supposed. At this point I was ready for anything. It was conversational hollering, perhaps, so I hollered back; "Hi, how ya' doin'?!"

We shouted at each other for a few minutes, and she told me that she was a Creole, and where she came from, and what it was like in the neighborhood, and how she was 'The Eye'. The rapid introduction came winding down to a halt. She looked at me suspiciously, and silent for a full minute – a peculiar pause, after so much yelling.

"Who are you?" She asked. "You know you might not be safe around here?"

I explained to her that I had just moved in.

"Oh, that's okay then… you seem like an alright guy." She had evaluated me rather quickly, with the same type of skill that I evaluated people who might want a taxi, but with a different style. She was boss lady around here. She knew wuz up, wit skillz.

In this neighborhood, where I lived now, where people didn't call the police-- there was something special going on to maintain order, and her name was Georgia.

Georgia was a great old lady, the ombudsman and arbitrator in this side of town. I don't think Georgia would ever hit anybody with that bat. It was symbolic, like a police officers badge. Nobody would mess with Georgia because the whole neighborhood backed her up. This old woman ran the block. I told her that my apartment had just been broken into. She said she'd keep an eye on the place, and I shouldn't have any more problems now that she knew who I was. In the long run, Georgia provided the most effective 'police services' that I'd ever experienced.

At first, I wasn't sure how effective Georgia would be, so I sought advice about home security from someone else. As a taxi driver in San Francisco I could find someone, who knew something, about any subject known to man. At one time or another there would be experts in every field visiting from everywhere in the world -- I just wanted to talk to a thief. "How do I keep a thief out?" I asked a few suspicious looking characters-- sometimes uneasy about my question. It may seem amazing that people would confess their crimes to cabdrivers, but they would, and I needed to know something. Not at all surprising to me, it didn't take long to find thieves who were eager to give me expert advice, proud that I would consult them about their profession. I was not going to be their victim, so they could redeem themselves in a way by acting like my hero for a moment.

One guy told me; "Locks only keep honest people honest -- and it depends on where you live, and who you know."

I responded; "I don't know you, and you don't know where I live."

"You might be lucky like that," he said, as I drop him off. I had already collected the fare in advance, of course.

Another fellow gave me more details; "Just have locks that keep things closed securely, like the hooks that you latch the screen door closed with, but make sure it stays shut tightly."

"That's it?" I asked.

"Yeah, if a window opens too easily, or if a door is ajar, it's like an invitation to come in."

"But those little wire hooks can be easily broken." "How would that keep anybody out?" I asked.

"Hey, if somebody really wanted to get in they could go through the wall with a chainsaw."

Alarmed by this story, I told it to other customers at random.

It didn't take long before someone told me; "Yeah, that happened to my friend. He came home from work, parked his truck in his garage -- he was tired, so he went in to go to sleep. While lying in his bed he heard a sawing, and assumed that a neighbor was cutting firewood or something. When he got up the next morning the entire back wall of his garage had been cut out and dropped into the rear alley. His truck, all of his tools, and everything that had been in his garage was gone."

After this bit of research I decided that an iron gate in front of a 3-inch thick door I had built, and bars over the previously offended window would be enough. Being under Georgia's wing was my real safeguard — It had to be.

Going back to the Tenderloin as just a visitor I grew to appreciate my new Lower Fillmore neighborhood, a place with a different flavor of distastefulness. To some people my neighborhood was more dangerous, and to outsiders that might be true, but I was finding a fit. In a ghetto away from the slums — I loved it. I saw too many problems in the Tenderloin that I often wondered how to address. I saw things that somehow other people were ignoring — horrible things. People didn't seem to notice, and I wondered why? When I went home I could forget about it. My neighborhood was somehow more manageable, more functional, and easier to think about.

Even still, I visited the Tenderloin almost every night, because, in a sense I had integrated myself into a social network there — I knew people too well, and felt it unethical to pretend I didn't know them just because they had problems.

I still felt ashamed that I hadn't taken time to talk to the kid who took his own life. How much trouble would a few minutes be for a kid who was asking for help? I wanted to make myself available. Too many children were involved in prostitution and other potentially destructive activities – other people didn't seem to see it. I knew too well that something was wrong. I didn't think I should look the other way. I'd keep an eye on the Tenderloin.

I saw Lisa on the corner around midnight. Lisa was a petite girl, about 5 feet tall, and rather slender. She was casually walking in a circle, as if the only way to find a way out of downtown would be to drill a hole to hell. She looked overworked and beaten, but trying to look cute. She was 13 years old. I had an idea...

I whipped the taxi around the block and pulled up to the curb by Lisa.

I called to her; "Come on, get in."

She hollered back; "I can't go anywhere."

"Just around the block," I said.

She looked around as if someone was watching, and said; "I shouldn't even be talking to you." She knew she could talk to me, because taxicabs were closely connected with the business of prostitution -- if that's what she was doing. As I got closer I could see that she had a black eye.

"OK, Just around the block," I told her, "Come on."

She seemed interested in my invitation to get off the corner for a minute, but looked around anxiously. Then she jumped in, and I quickly took off.

"I've got to get right back, or they'll kill me."

"Who will kill you?" I needed to know.

"The 'Outcasts' will kill me," she said.

I scoffed; "Oh, those punk kids trying to be big shots with their 'Outcast' gang?"

"Yeah," she said, and looked at me as if I wasn't taking it seriously enough.

"You need to get away from them."

"Easy for you to say," as she squinted her eyes and let out a sigh of frustration, then warned me; "You'd better watch out!"

"Come on with me. I'll take you to my new apartment."

"No way, I've got to go back!" "They'll kill me...they'll kill you!"

"No, I don't think so," I told her, "You can just blame me, and say I wouldn't take you back. It's not your fault; say the taxi driver wouldn't take you back, and they can kill me if they think they can."

She looked at me stunned, but seemed relieved to be able to shift the blame to me, and curious. She felt certain that I would be killed.

"You'll see, I warned you," she said. But she didn't really want to go back to the corner, and there was no way that I was going to bring her back there.

As we went into my apartment on Haight Street I showed Lisa the door I had built. It had four layers of 3/4-inch plywood bolted together -- secured with a half-inch thick steel hasp.

"Nobody can get to you through this," I told her.

She seemed impressed. I showed her around the large flat, gave her a blanket, and said that she could help herself to whatever she wanted in the refrigerator. I told her not to play with matches or anything like that as I headed for the door. She laughed, and looked comfortable watching TV, eating a banana. I had to go back to work.

She looked at me as if she wasn't going to see me again, and said; "Be careful."

When I returned later that night Lisa seemed surprised; "They didn't get you?"

"No, they aren't going to get me."

On the following day Lisa was still anticipating an attack by the juvenile street gang, and reminded me to lock the door when I left to work. I checked on her periodically during the night while driving across the city in my taxicab.

I had to figure out something to do with Lisa. She thought that she had to provide sex in exchange for me taking care of her, but that wasn't part of the deal. I needed help from one of the girls. Late in the night when I was driving through the tenderloin I saw Alice.

Alice was a feisty 16-year-old girl that was sort of a leader amongst the girl's her age on the streets. I pulled over to talk to her.

"Hey, Alice, I've got Lisa."

Alice approached my window to hear the news.

"The 'Outcasts' were forcing her to turn tricks on the corner, and she's got a black eye, but she's safe right now."

Alice was shaking her head; "I'd knock them out," she said. Alice had taken boxing lessons for years, and I'd seen her knockout guys on the street before. She wasn't kidding, and she knew that Lisa was easy prey.

"Alice, can you help?"

"What?"

"Come with me to see Lisa."

"Yeah, you're right, but what do you want me to do?"

"Just talk to her, and maybe find her a change of clothes."

"Yeah, I'd better, but I haven't got much time. Where is she?"

"She's over on Haight."

Alice jumped in, and I drove her to a room in the Tenderloin were she said she could pick up a change of clothes for Lisa.

Lisa was excited to see Alice come into my apartment when we got to the place on Haight. She was quick to say; "Don't tell them where I am."

"Tell who?" Alice said with a sneer. "I'll knock the shit out of them if they ask me any questions."

Little Lisa laughed and jumped up and down as Alice took her into the bathroom.

Alice had Lisa take a shower, got her cleaned up, and put new clothes on her.

"Hey, I've gotta go," said Alice. "Lisa, you'll be all right."

Lisa didn't say anything, and just stood there smiling. Alice had provide her with some sweat pants that were a little bit too large, a white T-shirt, and a windbreaker with sleeves that were at least 6 inches longer than her arms.

"Alice," I asked, "what's with that jacket you got? Did you think we needed something that could work like a straitjacket for Lisa?"

"I don't know, if we need to...," and Alice approached Lisa, acting as if she would tie the sleeves together on the jacket.

We had a quick laugh as we headed out. Alice wanted to hurry back to whatever she was doing, and I also needed to get back to work.

By the third day at my apartment Lisa had gradually become less surprised to see me return, still living. She was gaining confidence, forgetting the certain death promised by the street gang. I had made it clear to her that she didn't have to let people force her to work the streets. The spell of the 'Outcasts' had been broken. Now what? She had been telling me that she didn't know where her parents were. She became comfortable enough to tell, and finally revealed, that she actually had a mother with a phone number. I immediately handed her the phone and insisted that she call. She talked to her mother for about a half an hour -- for the first time in six months. The conversation seemed to go well. I wondered what her mother had been thinking and feeling about her daughter's disappearance. I asked if I could talk, and Lisa handed me the phone. I talked to Lisa's mother for awhile, and it appeared that a minor argument had led to Lisa running away, but home life didn't sound all that bad, and Lisa's mother definitely wanted her back home.

I told Lisa's mother that I would put Lisa on the Greyhound Bus. Soon after we got off the phone I was taking Lisa to the bus station in a final free taxi ride. An apparently successful mission motivated me. Yes, despite whatever trouble, I should talk to the kids. The lingering hint of guilt would be thus lifted. I felt that every person has a responsibility to contribute to the society in which they live, so; problems within our reach are somewhat our fault if they are ignored.

I risked the convenience of the taxi stand for parking, illegally abandoning the taxi while I went into the station, but just for a few minutes. I bought Lisa a ticket, made sure she got on the right bus, and watched to be certain that she left town. Lisa was on her way home. Afterwards, the 'Outcasts' would never say a word to me.

The taxi line hadn't moved by the time I came back. I pulled out, and sped off as if someone might still catch me -- getting away with a parking crime. Two other drivers who had pulled in behind me were glad to see me leave so they could move up a notch. I felt the mood of 'everybody wins' as I raced down the road, offsetting the dismal spirits of yet another slow Monday night. With no fares in sight, I saw a young man down the street, easy to notice because he had very long blond hair blowing in the wind. Not a potential fare, I deduced, but he reminded me of someone -- the kids engaged in curious mischief, from 4 years earlier, in the late night streets of Seattle. There was no mistaking that uniquely bright, incredibly long hair; moved by the ocean breeze that somehow forced its way, channeling down certain San Francisco streets like a wind tunnel. Convinced that I should talk to kids, and not having anything better to do, I pulled over to talk to him. I had a question anyway

"Hey, didn't I see you in Seattle?"

He stood at my window as I told him about street corners and clubs I thought I saw him hanging around some time ago.

"Was that you?" I asked.

He seemed awfully excited about the fact that I might have noticed him. Maybe he was high on something. In any event, if I was looking for someone who wanted to talk, I certainly found it. I let him get in the cab, and; relating to his past triggered an endless monolog. He proceeded to tell me his life story, or at least as much as I could bear, as we drove around for about 20 minutes. He was 14, so when I had seen him out all night on the streets in Seattle he had only been 10 years old! His parents divorced when he was 9. Confusion, and a feeling of rejection lead him to elect to make it on his own on the street, so he said. I thanked him for telling me about his life, and letting me know about things that went on during many a late Seattle night in the rain. I told him he was a cool guy, and if he ever need any help he could look for me, but I didn't want to be pestered - I'd do him one favor, just one — so save it for an emergency, I told him. But at the moment I had to get back to work.

"So, where do you want to go?" I asked.

"I want the favor now," he said, and then, as if it was another thought; "I want to show you where I live."

"Is that where you want to go right now?

"Yes."

He directed me to a residential hotel near Eddy and Leavenworth streets. He didn't say another word, except that his name was 'Kevin'. He didn't get to exactly what the favor was.

As hard as it is to find a parking place in San Francisco, nobody wanted the space right in front of this hotel, so we were quickly parked and out of the cab. Kevin motioned to the door, still silent, as I followed behind him.

There was a bum sitting near the doorway who was having difficulty asking a question -- as if I was fool enough to listen to a drunken request. As we entered the building I pressed against the far wall of the doorway in order to avoid the drooling vagrant.

Inside the lobby there was a musty smell with a piquant spiciness to it. We went up two flights of creaky stairs, and down a dusty hallway to a door that had come off the hinges. Kevin shook his head as if to put his long hair in place, and walked into the doorway with me right behind him. Beyond the broken door, a fat hairy man who looked like he was in his late thirties was standing there in boxer shorts.

"Where have you been, you were supposed to be here at 4:30!" The man yelled at Kevin, and then turned to give me a disgusting look as if I was a repulsive criminal; "You…" He sneered, but didn't finish his sentence. The fat hairy man seemed like he wanted to challenge me to a fight right there in his underwear, but he suddenly reeled around and landed sideways on the couch. Then I noticed that he had a hypodermic needle in his hand. I backed away. He could use that as a weapon. I looked around the room, and needles were strewn everywhere.

"This is where you live?" I asked Kevin quietly.

"Yeah, that's my roommate."

"Come on, let's go." I muttered.

Without another word Kevin followed me out of the building. The roommate was busy trying to get his fix. On the way out, the bum raised his hand and struggled to say something, but only said; "Uh oh", when he saw me jab Kevin with the spear hand to his chest.

"Kevin, you don't live here. Don't come back here." Kevin acted submissive, contrary to his normally aggressive demeanor. "Come on," I told him, and he got into the taxicab with me. I drove him a few blocks down the road, and dropped him off on Mason Street.

"What should I do?" asked Kevin, as he got out.

"Find some other place to stay, and if you can't, meet me right here at 4 a.m." I figured he'd find a place, or go back to the hellhole where he said he lived — but that was on him, at least I wasn't condoning it. He wouldn't meet me at 4, I thought, because it wasn't a very interesting place to wait, and there was no guarantee, in his mind, that I'd actually come back to get him. Then at 4 a.m. I drove down Mason Street just before I turned in the taxi, just because I said I would. I was surprised when, seeing me coming down the block, Kevin jumped up in the air like a rocket. He was there after all, so I took him home, fed him, and showed him where he could sleep.

The next morning I got Kevin to give me his parents phone number. They lived near Tacoma, about an hour south of Seattle. As I handed him the phone to make the call, Kevin told me that he didn't get along with his stepmother - "Don't talk to her," he said.

His dad answered the phone, and Kevin handed the phone to me. Right away I said; "I've got Kevin here in San Francisco, and I'll buy him a bus ticket and send him home."

Kevin's dad responded; "No, no, no, you keep him there and I'll send you money."

It seemed to me that there was something more than not getting along with his stepmother, so I found myself having a friendly conversation with Kevin's father for about an hour to see what was really going on. I gave him my address so he could send some money, because; he definitely didn't want Kevin back home.

After getting off the phone I turned to Kevin; "I don't really want a roommate, but you have no place to go, and your dad says that he'll send some money."

Kevin got happy, and I put my hand to stop him.

"No, I don't want a roommate, and you should find another place to stay that makes sense. If you show up here at 4 a.m. I'll let you sleep here, but you have to get up by noon and leave."

For about a month Kevin was waiting at my door every night when I came home from work. Finally, he said he found another place, a place in Pacific Heights, one of the richest neighborhoods in the world. I raised an eyebrow in disbelief, but it appeared to be true -- good for him. At the age of 14 he survived however he did, but he had been on his own since he was 9 or 10, and acted like he knew exactly what he was doing. His father never sent me a single dollar.

I dropped Kevin off at what looked like a $20 million mansion in Pacific Heights. He actually lived there now, so it seemed, but I often saw him in the tenderloin at night, anyway. His social network was Downtown. He could draw jealousy or admiration from his peers, and he in turn envied Ruben for some reason. I suspected that Kevin was a prostitute, but never asked.

Ruben, ever obsequious, and always praising me in front of everyone, had elevated me to hero status for rescuing Lisa, among other things. Now Kevin, adored by the other kids, was telling everyone that I was his brother. I became the notorious champion to the underdogs, and lots of kids started referring to me as 'Big Brother'. The title somewhat irritated me, because it appeared that George Orwell's frightening prophecy would become real, and the year of 1984 had arrived. It was a dreadful thought that our government could ever become so oppressive, and the movements of citizens scrutinized under a cameras eye. I'd be watching, but not to oppress. I would have been quite satisfied just watching, and telling other people about the trouble in the city, as if someone else was going to do something. But at this point I was the one, and there was no turning back.

On the street one day, Ruben ran over to me; "Hey, you got a minute, there's something you've got to see," he said.

"What?!" I said, irritated at attempts to distract me from the cab driving hustle.

"You won't believe it. I've got to take you to this place."

"Where??" I said impatiently.

"Over on Polk Street."

Ruben's dramatic appeal got me curious, and I asked him; "Can we do it later? I'm short shifting and I'm gonna turn in the taxi at nine o'clock."

The taxi garage was just a few blocks from Polk, and Ruben agreed to meet me there a little after 9.

At about 9:45 Ruben took me to an apartment that sat above a store on Polk Street. Ruben led me up the stairs and just walked right in the door. I followed behind him, and inside there was a woman screaming her head off, and swinging an iron by the cord like a gladiator with a weapon. She thrust the iron into a laundry basket like a final blow against an enemy. Dirty socks fell across the floor.

The woman froze to give a toothless smile, and said; "Hi Ruben," then quickly slipped around a corner into another room.

Ruben motioned me to sit on a couch with him. There were two boys in their early teens sitting in separate chairs against an adjacent wall. There was no other furniture in the room except a small table in front of the couch. The older brother had braces on his legs, and appeared to have other deformities. He had a bamboo stake in his hand, about 3 feet long, and a little thicker than a pencil. He was reaching over and poking his little brother, Mikey.

"Quit it," Mikey said, as he leaned away to avoid the stick.

The stick poked Mikey again and he shuffled his chair away a few inches.

"Mikey, quit jumping around in there," came a voice from the other room.

The stick poked again. Mikey jumped. The woman's head appeared around the doorway, screaming something.

Eyes wide and jaw dropped, I looked side-to-side, and then at Ruben.

"Just stay here a while," he said, as he abruptly got up and left.

Mikey was on his feet, and went into the room where the woman who liked to yell was doing something – she was his mother. I suppose it was the kitchen, because Mikey returned with a beer and set it on the little table in front of me. Oh, OK, I thought, I'll have a beer.

Mikey returned to his chair, got poked, rocked the chair, and the woman hollered again in a stern voice, "Mikey I told you...!"

As if I wanted whatever game this was to hurry up and end, I drank the beer rather quickly. Mikey casually walked back into the kitchen where his mother was doing something, and this time returned with both a beer and an ashtray. Beer and ashtray in front of me on the little table, I decided to have the beer and a smoke before I bounced out of this confusing scene. Halfway through my cigarette, the stick poking and screaming escalated. Mikey got up out of his chair and came over to me.

He leaned over, and in a desperate whisper asked; "Can you sleepover with me?"

I shook my head as if to wake from a nightmare, but before I could question his question, Mikey was already in the kitchen asking his mother; "Can he spend the night?"

She came out of the kitchen, saying; "It's time for you to go to bed anyway," and pushing against my back, as if I was just another one of her abused children, she marched us across the room to a ladder.

"Go on," she snarled. Lifting her arm as if to shove us up. I was in a state of confusion over everything that was happening, and glanced over my shoulder as if I was watching for an assailant.

The woman walked back towards the kitchen, and I followed Mikey up the ladder. Perhaps he would be in danger if I didn't stick around.

The ladder led up to a small loft. It appeared to be an area where a rather large HVAC system had once been, and somehow they got a bare mattress up there. There was hardly enough headroom to sit up.

"Mikey, what's going on around here?" I anxiously asked.

"My mother yells at me all the time, but I'm used to it."

One of Mikey's eyes was a little crooked and he explained to me that it was because his dad had socked him in the head when he was a baby. His mother always screams at him, and his dad beats the crap out of him. He said that his older brother was a birth defect, and he needed to go to a special hospital. "He gets spoiled," said Mikey.

Again without my asking, Mikey went down the ladder and returned with a beer. He continued his story, telling me that his parents said that they went to a lot of trouble to come from Kentucky, and had used up all of their resources to get their son the medical treatment he needed…

"They moved me to Polk Street," he said, "and told me to go out and make it on my own."

They did that? This area where Mikey lived was the number one spot-- known worldwide for child prostitution, especially boy prostitutes. After Mikey told me all this I immediately informed him; "I'll spend the night here with you, but we're going to get one thing straight."

"What's that?" He asked.

"We're both sleeping with all of our clothes on." I was glad to have had three beers to help me fall asleep. At least Mikey would be safe for one night.

Back on the street the following night I couldn't find Ruben. I heard from others that Mikey ran away. Good for him. I needed to talk to Ruben at some point to find out what else he knew about this crazy scene he led me to. Something had to be done, but not just with Mikey, society overall seemed to be heading in a strange direction—some sort of disease that I was having second thoughts about confronting.

No, I decided, I didn't care much about finding Ruben right away; he might have another kid 'I just had to meet'. There were hundreds of people at hand in all sorts of crisis situations—more than I could count. I should save myself with a fare out of the area. In other parts of town people weren't as likely to think that I was there to solve their problems, but I was too notorious in the Tenderloin. I needed a place to hide, and sometimes I wished I could just stay home and read all about it—instead of have reality slap me in the face.

Only a few people knew where I lived, but soon a mob would know. Up to fifty people between the ages of 13 and 23 would show up at my door every day. This was no hiding place for me. The phone rang continuously. I wasn't going to do any reading. I had to put a stop to this tidal wave of the downtrodden. Besides, what would people think? I had kidnapped a 13-year-old girl and kept her prisoner for a few days. I had a sleep over with a 13-year-old boy. People would certainly think I was up to something devious, and some people already did. If I was testing for the limits of fearlessness, this was getting too scary. Particularly because I had met four teenagers who had told me about men who were in prison for molesting them, and how they had given testimony about the men who hadn't actually done anything.

One of the accusers, a boy, seemed to feel powerful for putting a guy in prison for 15 years, and said he didn't even know the alleged assailant until his mother pointed him out. His mother insisted upon what the man must be up to, and told her son what to say. This seemed to be not so uncommon: A girl actually gave me a four-page statement providing the details of how a babysitter had told her that she would never see her family again if she didn't say what she was told to say. The babysitter tormented the girl by having her rehearse statements implicating an innocent man.

The man, after serving 10 years in prison was paroled, but then violated when his parole officer saw a child safety seat in his car after he'd loaned the car to someone. A condition of his parole was that he couldn't have any contact with children. He didn't even know the child seat was in his car, and never even saw the child that sat in it—if there ever was one. The guy hadn't done anything wrong in the first place. The guy is still in prison even though his alleged victim had taken a sworn statement recanting her original testimony to both the DA, and a private attorney, in an attempt to resolve her guilt over the conviction of an innocent man. I decided that with all this I'd better secure a hideout before I really needed one.

A massive lock held fast on the front door, and I went through three doors to go in the back way. I wasn't about to try to answer the door, and trusted that the knocking would eventually cease. I piled up a stack of books about everything from ancient civilizations to modern media, and pretended I wasn't home. I wanted to see street people only when I was in the streets. I'd keep my social life in the taxicab. It's like I had jumped into a pile of garbage, right in the middle of it, and kicked it around to find what was really there. But I had to get out of it and brush myself off -- before I looked dirty, or even became a piece of garbage myself. I had enough excitement on the street, and I enjoyed being home alone reading. I also started writing, keeping a log of some of the events that occurred in the taxi:

Tuesday, July 17: A drunk gave me a big hassle and then shortchanged me. I chased him down the street and smacked him upside the head as a security guard watched.

Wednesday, July: 18: Alejandro Calderon, high on drugs, says he's leaving for 90 days to Mexico to become a rock star... claims he met some rich guy who is sponsoring him. I simply told him; "No, don't do it."

Thursday, July 18: Cab #379 bounced up and down and swayed back and forth. A spring in the seat ripped a customer's suit. I took the cab to the shop and short-shifted at 9:20.

Friday, July 20: I figured my skill had moved up a notch when I found myself caught in the middle of a six car pileup on the freeway, and somehow slipped through it without a scratch … Late in the evening, in front of a Chinese restaurant, I saw two waitresses, and a cook, all attacking a queer who frantically blew his 'gay protection whistle' to no avail.

Saturday, July 21: I left the lock off of the front door of my apartment. Richard came over early. Al came over. Dino came over with a friend from Michigan. Michael came over and tried to give me cocaine. Kim and Nancy came over. Larry and Tony came over. Tony got in an argument with Kim by calling her bitch. Michael gave Al some cocaine and Al started going crazy. Jehovah Witnesses stopped by, and I said, "Come on in!" I'll remember to keep the lock on the door from now on.

The phone was still ringing, and I had to put a stop to that, too. I bought a very expensive answering machine. Not that I needed an expensive one, but the issue was so important that paying a higher price made me feel better. I posted a very long message on the answering machine, extracted from the writings of a man whose name was not a name in all, and just means 'Old Man'. The writings have been revered for over 2500 years, but in all that time it doesn't seem that people got the message. I amused myself by making people listen to an announcement of at least a full minute before they could leave a message, for example:

"The moving force of the universe is nameless because it includes all things.

That which can be named is limited to things within our grasp.

Yet, we reach for the unfathomable, the incomprehensible, the inexplicable, and

seek to hold the secrets of life in a container we can call on like a friend.

We hold up the packaging with pride, yet hold up an empty shell -- it becomes us.

A container itself has no real value except for the substances it can hold.

When we identify a thing of beauty as such, we open our eyes to also recognize

ugliness. When we acknowledge goodness as such, then evil becomes reality.

Weight and weightlessness cannot exist without each other.

To know the secrets we must quiet our mind.

If we wish to hold the secrets as a possession they will escape us, and we will be

left holding an empty jar.

Therefore, to know the truth; be still, and look over your environment -- not

naming, not desiring, and passing no judgment.

Ride the force with loving calm, not wanting, because all is there.

You cannot contain it because it contains you.

Be there with it, and it will whisper it secrets.

Partake in serenity.

Cling to nothing.

Out of nothing a new spirit will rise."

My interpretation of the Tao Te Ching served as a wall in my phone that few people would jump over. The phone became silent before the knocks on the door would stop, but the harshness of the neighborhood was enough to deter people from hanging around long when there was no answer. Eventually the surge of would-be visitors subsided. It had to stop, because a couple of people went so far as to whisper their suspicions to people I knew—that I was like Charles Manson, Jim Jones, or some other mass murderer in the making. Was it because of my answering machine? They didn't know anything.

There was too much that the public didn't know, and wouldn't know in the face of a treacherous media bent upon playing with people's emotions. People want to put labels on things in order to establish a reference, and feel they have a handle on the world—for this the media plays with people's minds. The media has too much influence, and influence hardly placed to solve any problems – they'd profit more by sending us on a wild goose chase if it would keep us watching. Media was not just radio & television and such; it had extended itself to the back of milk cartons—There was no escape.

The milk carton scare could serve as a dramatic example of what the larger media does (to defy the claim that they have no influence). A whole generation was growing up that had been exposed to this new medium -- wanted posters on milk cartons. Never before had advertising been seen on milk cartons; suddenly there was, and it got a lot of attention-- especially since it was about kidnapped children. Children and mothers were terrorized by this, and assumed that stranger abductions were occurring everywhere. The media's love of witch-hunts and lynch mobs was making it dangerous to even talk to kids.

It took years before it would be clarified that the people kidnapping these children were their own parents! We don't even seem to notice the harmful effect to children -- being further detached from adults by this. We are so detached — oblivious to it, why?

If posters on milk cartons could shift society in such a way, what do you think the TV and video games have done? Violence in video games in Japan might not have much of a negative effect, so they say, but Japan had an impeccable culture that was unchanged for almost 2000 years. Show the same violence to angry Mexicans, and you'd better expect shootouts in the streets. Even Japan is building a time bomb for itself. Media does have influence. A trigger may have been just pulled in your own head because of it, but you never notice the many moments within your day when this happens — when the effects of brainwashing kicks in — ever so subtly.

The media likes the idea of random 'unexplainable' acts -- in hopes to keep people on the edge of their seat, and eager to tune in at the next opportunity for more bullshit--along with an announcement, of course, about what's supposed to be your favorite kind of soap or something. Ad driven media is dangerous, the legacy of Dr. Watson — a pioneer in the development of the field of psychology -- who subjected babies to torture, but got booted from academic life on account of a sex scandal (never mind his experiments with babies and small animals). Watson went on to apply his mastery at manipulation to the advertising industry, and developed the style that persists to this day. An often-malicious adjunct to the media, and the driving force of the all-seeing ever-present God of modern times used by unscrupulous manipulators to tell us what we want, and how to think, and literally drive the masses like stupid cattle. The monstrous reach of advertising had even gone so far as to find a place on milk cartons -- to invoke fear in us in the midst of breakfast. Would your kids get kidnapped today?

Such a large number of parents kidnapping their own children was a relatively new phenomenon—reflecting a change in society. It used to be, that when a couple got together, they might not even kiss for a few months. Don't you think it would be important to take the time to find out if you can even be friends first? But then, contrary to longstanding convention, more than half of all marriages in these modern times end in divorce within three years. The way romance was being handled seemed to explain the picture with so many damaged kids.

There were many clues as to why society had gone awry. Media sound bytes had sparked a lot of it, and gone perhaps to a point of no return, as it fostered so much simplistic thinking. Perhaps the only solution would be to start over – we could look forward to everything falling apart. I would look to my customers for more clues, and answers. It was too much to think about, especially since my own thinking had no doubt been twisted in some way by the very thing I hoped to investigate. My mind reeled with thoughts about the realities of the world, continuously adding to the catalog of ideas – one customer to the next.

While cruising the Tenderloin, a girl flagged me down. I didn't know her. She wanted to go to the Mission District, and from the looks of her she just got some money, and she was either going to go home with it, or go spend it on drugs, I guessed. The part of the Mission where she was going had cheap rent, and lots of dope. I knew she was a prostitute, and trying hard to make sure it didn't sound personal, I thought I'd play some kind of good citizen role – by some morality I inadvertently believed. I talked about the evils of prostitution, in a very general way, as to not so bluntly accuse her of anything.

As I was dropping her off-- in response to my apparently self-righteous sounding lecture, she said;

"Hey look buddy, all women are prostitutes-- some of them just marry their tricks." As she left, I reminded myself, again, that I should shut up sometimes.

The dispatcher was calling for a cab on Albion Street, a couple of blocks from where I was dropping off. I grabbed the microphone, and took a call for a pickup at a bar. No one else was interested in this one, known for patrons so drunk that cabbies would joke; "You have to pour them into the cab." Within moments I was at the bar, and a woman with a large purse jumped into the cab to be followed by a gentleman -- after he finished payment of a bill in the bar. I couldn't help but think about the statement by the prostitute I had just dropped off, and wondered how it might apply to these customers.

The obviously inebriated couple said that they wanted to go to Berkeley. I gave the gentleman a cold stare for a moment, which invited his assurance of the ability to pay.

"Don't worry, I've got you covered," he said.

He didn't look too drunk to be reasoned with, but I continued to scrutinize the character of my passengers, as is always prudent.

An apparent argument ensued between the couple.

"I've been waiting for you all my life," said the gentleman.

The woman snapped back; "No you haven't! You only met me two weeks ago. You only have been waiting two weeks."

The quarrel quick-shifted to kiss and make up, and what seemed to be an over dramatization of the passions of foreplay. While crossing the Bay Bridge, something caught my eye in the middle of the rear view mirror, and I looked up to see the woman's leg in the air -- a golden glittered high-heeled shoe dangling from her toe. Soon we were exiting the freeway in Berkeley.

The couple sat up, and the woman made some comment to the man about how he didn't have money, then she made it clear several times that she had no money either, i.e., he'd better have money.

I indicated that the fare was $39, and the woman, who didn't appear to have the capacity to see straight, began to make a scene about the fact that the meter only said $35.

The guy, who understood that there was a bridge toll, and hopefully a tip, couldn't care less -- he was trying to find his wallet.

The woman began screaming, "Let's go!"

The man became visibly distressed as he searched his pockets, as well as the back of the cab several times, with the result of giving me only $25. Finally, after more searching, with the woman escalating to viciousness, he found his wallet under the seat; quickly handed me two $20 bills, and was gone before I could ask if he wanted change, or his $25 back, or his credit cards that he dropped on the way out ... more food for the lost and found.

Comparing the barroom encounter, and a date with a prostitute raises a question about the complexity of how things must be partitioned. One woman demands a specific amount of money, while another is somewhat vague, but still makes it clear that the gentleman must pay. Is it the influence of money, or media, or should these things even be considered as part of the formula? Is sex the most important part of a relationship? I had questions.

Romance is an important part of the big picture, but I wanted to study every aspect of civilization to figure out what was going on.

To effectively analyze human interaction there are several factors to consider: There is government, and profit-seekers, and media, and education, and criminals, and both the natural and un-natural propensities of people, and so many other things — it's too much to view at once, but all things must be considered in order to get a clear picture.

To look at one thing at a time can skew the conclusion, but; we have to start somewhere, and sex is an important issue.

In the animal Kingdom creatures might forgo food at the chance opportunity for sex. Only after the necessities of survival are well established might the possibilities of creative endeavors occur—but sex trumps all. How much have animal instincts been pushed out of proportion in human life? Certainly there has been manipulation, pairing products with sex for corporate gains, and laying cultural values to waste in stagnation—truly a rape of the mind. I wanted to consider the whole picture, and at the same time I wanted to forget it all, and just go along with thinking about sex, or shopping all day. I decided I'd stay home and read about the roots of civilization - to see if I could.

I had open books piled all over my apartment, and evaluated what I read through discussions in my taxicab. When out of the cab I spent most of my time alone, studying. After a few months of this I was ready for more trouble, and began to miss having a girl around all of the time. I dreamed of being like a lot of guys who have a wife. But, with popular culture bent upon sex we might as well not even have an institution of marriage, and I decided, after a lot of thought, that I should have three girlfriends. It seemed to be a great idea the more I tried to rationalize it. A couple of girls had caught my eye.

Whatever I was studying... The notion occurred that sex had been overemphasized as an evil diversion that I hoped to expose, but ironically, my interest in studying social structures got completely derailed by a sex goddess.

Misty, a magnificent vixen who worked as an exotic dancer, was visiting me with two other girls. Nancy, an aggressive girl that preferred the company of women to men, and Mary, a prostitute that liked to pretend that she was not a whore at all.

The three of them were together so much that they were often referred to collectively as 'MNM'. In the mix of the many whores I could list as friends, these were some of my favorite girls, but every young girl on the street seemed to be in love with me. I decided it was time to put the books down and take advantage.

Sex was all over the media, serving to influence us all, and; according to the media impressions, some of the girls I knew looked upon their lifestyle as glamorous. I too was hooked into some electronic fantasy, perhaps, and led to believe that having three girlfriends would be the thing to do. Having an exotic dancer, a stripper, and a hooker as housemates should elevate my status in contemporary society — of course. We were all friends, and we might make it better with some benefits. Why not? Unlike so many relationships; they could do what they want, and I could do what I want. These girls had things to do, and it was none of my business. They'd come home to me and I had nothing to bother them about; they understood I needed sex. If one of the girls had a headache that was OK as long as it didn't get contagious. These girls knew very well -- guys need sex, so we could skip the bullshit. We got along fabulously, in my opinion.

The women would come and go as they pleased. They didn't have to pay rent, and the freezer was full of filet mignon. I was a friend they could feel safe with. I would listen, and they could tell me about some frustrating situation that they had to deal with, and I knew exactly what they were talking about. There were no complex rituals to endure for taking care of my needs, and they had no problem with it; perhaps, because it was a shared duty. I took care of them, and they took care of me. After about three months, having a relationship with three women seemed to work better than some relationships that I've had with just one partner.

For some reason, I decided that adding a fourth girlfriend would be the thing to do. The open and honest relationship seemed to be working so well, and I had interest in another girl—so why not have four girlfriends? I thought that she would certainly get along with the other girls, and there was no objection to moving her in. I assumed that the shared duty of serving me would defy any protest. Four girlfriends…that'll work… and it seemed like a smooth transition toward what many guys might only dream of.

After a couple of weeks of the five of us together there seemed to be a hint of confusion in the air. I didn't know if there was a problem. If some conflict was about to erupt, it was suspended by a variety of diversions -- I redecorated the apartment, painted an entire wall with brilliant black light paint, installed disco lights, and put in an extraordinary sound system. I wanted to enhance the atmosphere for the perpetual party I had going on with my girlfriends.

We were having such a good time; why not invite another woman to the party? I'd met yet another gal that I took fancy to, and everybody had a good time when I brought her over to meet the other girls. So… now I had five girlfriends.

With the six of us living together things soon changed. Sometimes it seemed like there was some strange plot going on that I didn't understand. Sometimes I felt like I was on another planet.

One of the girls had a guy come by to deliver a package, or something. He saw the apartment fixed up like a nightclub, with Misty dancing naked on the table, and three other girls sitting around in their underwear. After witnessing this, the news that I was running my own private orgy spread like wildfire. Some Playboy image about me spread beyond the normal boundaries of social networks, and some men who I would never suspect, went out of their way to meet me -- extending peculiar admiration.

Five girlfriends suddenly seemed almost too many, and I came to figure, from the way people were acting, that when Kings had large harems, that they didn't have sex with them all -- they just held them to intimidate other men. I just wanted the other men to stay away. If I could have five girlfriends... I'd like that, and find a way to adjust, but I didn't have any use for publicity. I was pleased, however, that the publicity drew out a volunteer to be number six. Oh, why not?

I had six girlfriends for less than a week, and suddenly the situation exploded.

Kim told me; "I kicked Debbie out because she said she was going to get in good with you and keep you all for herself."

Misty started screaming at me; "I loved you, and you let me down."

I didn't know what she was talking about.

Lorraine said; "I'm sick of this," and just walked out with her backpack and a paper sack.

I very quickly went from six girlfriends to none at all. There was no argument. Nobody was really mad at me, but suddenly we didn't all live together anymore. I was left completely alone at home, with nothing but a story to tell.

All alone in an apartment set up for a party, with lights flickering and the music blasting, I sat there by myself, thinking. I had an idea that I called 'Quadrogamy'. If two women and two men could all get married to each other -- nobody would have to cheat, and; who could abuse a women if another man was also her husband? There seemed to be some merit to this notion. Taking note of some of the problems I encountered, I speculated on how such a deal might work better. There might be economic benefits, and everything. Perhaps such an arrangement would be appropriate for a new era. It was more to talk to people about in the taxi.

I could research the oddest things in the taxi. I often relished getting different sides of a story, and could meet people of all kinds. I met famous actors, scientists, and politicians. When I thought I might like playing a clarinet or sax; I met a clarinetist from the Cleveland Orchestra, Benny Goodman's chauffeur, Lester Young's son, and Woody Herman himself.

I had a question about the word apartheid, because I had been to an apartheid rally and couldn't find anyone who could tell me with the word really meant. What better chance to get an answer than to meet of former member of South African Parliament? He was traveling America incognito with a French passport. He actually stayed with me as a houseguest for three days, and explained all sorts of details that I'd never heard of before. I came to the conclusion that whatever goes on in South Africa was none of my business -- or anyone else's that isn't living there, I suppose.

I also had questions about the Middle East, and was invited to dinner by the son of an Arab Sheik. He took interest because I'm obsessed with critical thinking. He claimed that I couldn't possibly be an American, and curious, asked me to remain with his entourage for the rest of the evening. His group surrounded me at the dinner table and bombarded me with an Arab viewpoint I had never heard before.

To learn about politics... I also enjoyed the opportunity to spend many hours with Elmer Robinson talking in the taxi. Robinson, who had been mayor of San Francisco from 1948 to 1956, was also the president of the National Council of Mayors. He was an expert on political systems throughout the history of the United States. What better person to talk with about politics? On one occasion he told me that he knew Dianne Feinstein since she was a little girl, and didn't understand what she was doing as mayor.

He said that when he was mayor, he would direct his efforts at what he called 'the little people' --waiters, and hairdressers, and people like that, who might be struggling to make ends meet. He tried to bring about a spread of conventions throughout the year, and do whatever he could to uplift the people who were struggling on the bottom. The people on the top didn't need any help, he said. In our last conversation before he died, he seemed distressed by the changing times, and said that he didn't understand. I learned a lot from him, but he had some questions himself about how things were going in the wrong direction.

The things I could learn from customers were far-reaching, so I figured it shouldn't be so hard to study something so common as having lovers. I asked people about the idea of having more than one lover at a time, and it turned out that quite a lot of people did -- they cheated. From what I gathered, it was not too uncommon to maintain as many as three lovers for a while. Four lovers at once was somewhat unusual, and people who claimed to have five lovers often provided descriptions which only made them sound like liars. I evaluated the claims, and the descriptions had to fit with what I was sure to be true. I believed I could sort the bullshit. It appeared from the stories that I was told, that; an ongoing relationship with more than four people, intimately involved, didn't come easy (Duh?). I concluded that the maximum number of lovers, which an ordinary person could maintain under any circumstances, would be six. Of course, to do that wouldn't be very ordinary, but I had a few rather ordinary people provide believable descriptions of maintaining relationships with as many as six lovers.

To give an example of what I found convincing was a story of one old man. I had known him for a while, and suspected that he had ongoing relationships with several women...

I asked him about it, and he described the system -- with emphasis on a few points... 1) He never brought any women to his house, because they might run into each other there. 2) He had women in different towns, and it was easy for him to say that he was out of town most of the time. 3) If he had a girl that he only saw on Tuesday, he had to be diligent about seeing her every Tuesday. This is what he said, and I wanted to see, so; I offered the old man free rides to go about his rounds with the girls in town, which he was glad to accept -- and pleased to allow me to witness his playboy antics. Over the course of a couple of months he took the cab and picked up his dates in the city of Pacifica, and in Millbrae, as well as a couple of women in San Francisco. He suddenly had a third woman in San Francisco, and informed me that he periodically had to refresh his list of women, and replace one with a new acquaintance from time to time. He claimed he had maintained six girlfriends for years, but now he had seven, and appeared to be having a problem about deciding which one to dismiss. He seemed to think that seven was too many (Oh, really?) and I don't know how it worked, but he had seven girlfriends for about three weeks... Then, suddenly I sensed a turmoil developing throughout his life. He finally eliminated one of the girls, getting back to six, but evidently the move came too late -- the old man who had to an elaborate system to maintain six girlfriends for several years suddenly went from six to zero. His system seemed to work for a long time, at least with older women, but it totally fell apart when he went beyond a certain limit. It didn't seem to matter whether there was a system or not, younger or older people, deceitfulness, or an open and honest relationship; the threshold of chaos, for intimacy, appeared to be around the number six. I compared this data with scientific research by Calhoun.

Functional limits differ according to the character of the engagement.

Six might be the maximum for real intimacy, but larger numbers could function efficiently with other types of social interaction.

In John C. Calhoun's 'Mouse Universe', when the general population exceeded 150, a condition we can define as chaos occurred, and then no adjustment within the society of mice made a difference any more.

A dysfunctional environment might accelerate with any population increase, along with the tendency is to cope with it, but coping only stalls the inevitable. Eventually the mouse universe was disrupted, and then sent on an inexorable course to total extinction. It didn't matter if the mice were contained in a relatively small pen, or could roam a quarter acre-- it was the number of individuals that they had to interact with that made the difference. For the mice, more than 150 individuals became too much to attend to, or think about. Perhaps the mice also had subgroups, but we can't really know what mice are thinking.

Thoughts of mice and men had sent me off on a tangent, extending the theory of terminal chaos from the most intimate relationships to social interactions with larger numbers, and in various formats -- to conclude, that: The threshold of chaos is relative to the intensity and design of an engagement.

I tried to speculate upon how the threshold of chaos might apply within various parameters of human interaction. There was a drug dealer, who had for a while maintained a network of over 150 sub-dealers. His organization had 4 supervisors who each had 4 agents, who in turn each distributed to 7 small dealers. The numbers seemed to fit my other evidence. Especially interesting, was when this dope dealer decided to expand his operation. Suddenly, one of his managers broke away, and like a house of cards the entire operation quickly fell into chaos. Later I saw the dope dealer, who had run a little empire for while, selling nickel bags on a street corner by himself.

As group size increases there is an urge to divide up. For example, with phone numbers we find it comfortable to deal in groups of three and four numbers. If you think about it, people only really learn how to count to 10. Even God is said to have needed a rest after six days. In order to maintain functionality, as the numbers within a group increase, it is necessary to know how and where to provide partitioning.

According to the value of a group size there are limits on how much we can think about. With the most intimate things the number may be similar to how many items we can identify at a glance – without counting.

I had known what it's like to have too many people to think about. Twenty visitors in a day had been a bit much, but I could deal with that. When 50 or more people started showing up my door every day it drove me crazy. On a more intimate level, seven people set off a bomb that left nothing standing. I could deal with all the crazy nonsense the world had to offer in the cab by separating the world I met with at work from my quiet time at home alone. I could see a reason why Romulus killed his brother for tearing down a wall he built.

The police provided an extra incentive for me to maintain boundaries against the world at large. Or so I was inspired, when one day I was called to come into the taxi garage in the middle of my shift. Upon parking in the taxi garage to see what it was about, I was quickly surrounded by a group of armed officers. There was a question about Lisa. I was asked to go downtown and talk to a detective.

"Where is Lisa?" asked the detective.

"I don't know, why are you asking me?"

"Her mother said that you were a friend of hers, and she ran away again, so she might have come back to you."

"She was never with me. All I had to do with her was get her away from a street gang that was forcing her into prostitution. I bought her a bus ticket and sent her back to her mother."

"Well, she ran away again. Do you know anything about her?"

"No, I never really had anything to do with her."

"Do you know that she's only 14, and what could happen to you for fooling around with a minor?"

"She was only 13 when I sent her back home, and I didn't fool around about it."

"You could get yourself in a lot of trouble. There are agencies to deal with these things, and you should leave it to them."

"OK, can I go now?"

The interview was over, and I ran out of the police station and got back in my cab.

A whole wastebasket full of laws were designed to protect Lisa, but her belief in her peers was far more powerful.

Evidently, she didn't have good communication with her mom, either. There may have been other deficiencies in social interaction around the town she was from. Hometown life might have been boring; she may have lacked encouraging friends, no feeling of purpose, and, perhaps; an invitation to a wild life 'as seen on TV', or something else inspired her to run away – it wasn't me. Whatever it was, something wasn't working for her -- so much that she'd face the risk of departing into the unknown, rather than enjoy the safety and security provided by a good parent. She needed to build her own wall somewhere perhaps? I didn't know.

I shouldn't have bothered, "There are agencies," said the rather gruff detective. He didn't have any solutions in his pocket, so why be so caustic about public involvement?

There was only one official agency in town that was designed to deal with problems like Lisa had, and that agency, ironically, was located just half a block from the corner where she had worked as a prostitute.

I decided it was definitely best to keep my social life on the streets, and drive by fast sometimes in order to avoid a call to socialize. I'd rather be home alone studying Calhoun's Rats than sticking my nose in a garbage can. Given my real world encounters, my quiet time at home studying dysfunctional socials systems through books was getting real exciting. I began to consider a fundamental pretense, in that; relationships between just two people are basic to all human interaction. Before I went any further looking at larger groups -- I decided that the question I should ask was: What makes a marriage work?

To explore how relationships work I interviewed several dozen elderly couples whom had been together for 40 years or more, and asked them: "What made your marriage endure?" To this question I got only two answers, with most of the couples telling me that the reason for success in their marriage was that "they had exactly the same interests", and the rest said that they "left each other alone". Some gave both answers: "They had exactly the same interests, or left each other alone."

In order to conduct the research I guessed where people with the answers might be, and just made myself available. I could simply park in front of a dance for seniors, or cruise in neighborhoods where there were many elderly residents. I looked for events that might attract the elderly, or when looking for a fare—just look for an elderly couple as a preference. One time, for example, when a crowd of people had been waiting a long time, and people were ready to fight each other for a cab, I got out, locked the doors, and announced; "Mr. & Mrs. Herbert", and walked into the crowd.

I picked out an elderly couple, and softly said; "You're not Mr. & Mrs. Herbert, but you look like you're happily married?"

"Oh, yes, we've been married 40 years."

That was good enough for me, and I told them; "These people are crazy, and at this moment I'd like to pick up someone who knows how to get along. I'll just call you 'The Herberts' for a moment, and get you away from this madness, if you don't mind."

"Oh, please do!"

This wasn't so unusual, because when there is a mob trying to get a cab, sometimes waiting for a long time, the mob mentality becomes most offensive. The person who declares "I'm first" is often the last person I'd want to pick up — they are pushy against a crowd, and if I let them in my cab they'll try pushing me around. No, I'll decide who's first, and picking an elderly person in the background might be the appropriate thing to do anyway. From various venues, in time, I found plenty of elderly couples who had been married for decades.

With information from 59 elderly couples, I discussed the results with many more people I met in the cab, and considered my conclusions reliable. The results of this study were that: Thirty-three (33) couples, the majority, claimed that having exactly the same interests was the key to success in their marriage; Nineteen (19) couples said that when they didn't have exactly the same interests, they left each other alone, and; Five (5) people said that their marriage endured simply because of the single factor-- they left each other alone. When asking people who had successful marriages of 10 or 20 years I got a variety of answers... "It's because of honesty."... "It's because of our extended family."... "It's because of how we met"... and so on, but; people who had been married 40 years or more only had two answers, either: 1) We have exactly the same interests, or; 2) We leave each other alone. Many people had both answers combined.

People can remain happily married for a long period of time if they have the same interests, but not just interests at the level of animal instincts, not just for rudimentary necessities like food and shelter; personal interests must go beyond what is given as almost universal.

The idea of a need for people to leave each other alone can be extended to politics, and other things. If majority rules, the majority may think that everyone should be the same, because they themselves had not yet recognized the need for an alternative. Hey, leave each other alone! Other people may really need the option of leaving each other alone, and herein lays an apparent defect in the idea of democracy. For the sake of truth I relished contrary views. In my quest to unravel the secrets of society's ills I frequently intersected the unfriendly topics of race religion and politics.

Religions had something to say about marriage, of course, and some religions claim to say something about everything. Religion represents the foundation, and driving force of many cultures, so religion can't be ignored in a comprehensive study of human behavior and society. Many religions were based on rules, reinforced ideas about obedience, or appeared to be to have been designed as forms of government. From the perspective of group size that I had been taking, it appeared that a need for religion might have occurred in ancient times to bring about order in the face of chaos. But instead of bringing real solutions, it served to perpetuate a dysfunctional system, and made it functional only according to it's own confinements. There is, allegedly, a vindictive guy in the sky who wrote the rules in the sand with his finger, and will cast you in a pit of fire for eternity if you don't obey. The promise of heaven, on the other hand, makes a pathetic existence in the present life more bearable. I consider religion to be sometimes scary, but people want to believe.

Belief will uplift a person from a feeling of helplessness... as would occur when chaos looms. When there is too much to think about we just don't process some of the data, and our world may seem to come apart. Confusion may be compounded as we look for outside sources, some authority -- and in ancient times religion provided relief in this manner. Some religions had 10 commandments, and along with the model of the judgmental God — courts were established to levy punishments based upon a language of absolutes, as if coming from God, and the court acted as an arm of God.

Dysfunctional systems are hard to change, and even though we know that their power doesn't come directly from God, the court system carries on with the act to this day — wielding so much power according to absolutes — as if ordained by an all knowing, all powerful being, above mankind.

Other ancient religions had a heaven that required death in battle for admittance. Needless to say, they didn't need to write down any rules — Even to tell a lie might be considered a challenge to fight to the death. From this alternative, a culture developed that was too honest to easily detect trickery, and fell prey to manipulators with their rule books. All of these ideas about the moving forces of culture may be interesting, but don't easily resolve to a conclusion... especially when we have been compelled to cope with silly things for so long. I grew weary of digging through the pile of ancient texts piled upon my kitchen table.

I could easily trash the idea of Heaven and Hell in favor of the Law of Conservation of Matter - a scientific principal of Chemistry and Physics that more-or-less says that you can't create of destroy anything that exists, only change its form.

If you burn a piece of wood the elements don't go away; hydrogen and oxygen goes into the air and carbon is left behind. At some point those elements are being put together to make another piece of wood or something.

I didn't believe in the God that would favor you if you only knew his real name, or agree with the people that claimed they know what planet God lives on, etc. No, the idea of a God that is a person may have served kings in administering their rule, but it didn't suit me. I'd rather consider that everything is a part of God, not a separate being, but every thing that exists is like a cell in the body of God. People who thought they might be entirely separate in themselves might be like cancer cells. Whatever...I was seeing things differently when I looked at it from the view of functional groups, cognitive limits, and what people do in the face of chaos. I grew distressed about how people would cling to some beliefs. I needed to drop the study and get outside. I threw down the books and headed for the door.

I didn't want to go far away, just away from the books for a while, so I just set a bistro table on the sidewalk in front of the window of my basement apartment.

I brewed an herbal tea with Chamomile, Licorice root, Cascara Sagrada, Chickweed, and Yellow Dock. This concoction might be called for to have a calming and cleansing effect. After stuffing myself with edicts and rituals for several days I felt full of crap – the tea was a personal joke, as if I needed a mild laxative. It was something different to do, and I set a teapot and a couple of mugs on the bistro table.

Fluffy clouds decorated the clean looking sky, and looking down the block of Victorians -- it was a beautiful place -- sitting at the bistro table sipping tea I could relish a lovely day. Looking at it all as if everything was like a cell in the body of God made it easy to contemplate unconditional love.

There was little activity in the neighborhood, as I sat at the bistro table on the sidewalk in front of my apartment window, sipping tea. I sat quietly, doing nothing, just watching--It felt good.

One block down-- Fillmore Street --had been like an African-American vain that went through a section of the city, away from the shipyards where most black people lived. On Fillmore Street lived an old woman named Sapphire.

Sapphire still complained about her husband, deceased now for 20 years: "He said he was out to sea, out to sea; yeah, out to see some other woman at the Rat Trap Bar downtown." Sapphire still complained about him, and it was all she could say to her older brother when he came from Louisiana on account of their daddy's funeral. Their daddy had come from Louisiana to work in the shipyards -- he lived to the age of 99. Sapphire's brother, Leroy, had always stayed in Louisiana, and didn't like coming to San Francisco, even now-- especially to hear his little sister goin' on about some long dead deadbeat husband of hers.

I saw the silhouette of a stick figure moving cantankerously down the sidewalk from the corner of Fillmore. The stick figure slowly drifted closer, with cane in hand actively groping for stability. As Leroy hobbled toward my bistro table I asked if he'd like to sit down for tea.

Leroy was glad to have the opportunity to sit down. I poured him a mug of tea, but he didn't drink much of it. He told me about his father, and his sister, and how he didn't take much liking to it here -- The City was too busy. He had come here once before, years ago, but went back home, and never again left Louisiana. He lived in small town on the outskirts of Baton Rouge all of his life.

"My dad liked working in the shipyards, and stayed around here even after they shut down and he couldn't find work anymore. The government had shipped black folks all over to work in ship yards and things, and then left them hangin' when the job was over -- put them in housing projects if they stuck around. I figured it better to stay down home. I went back home and started a beer delivery business," he said.

"Is that right, how did that go for you?"

"It was pretty good. I had it going on for many years, raised a family, and put my daughter through college. She's a nurse now."

"How'd you happen to get into that business?" I asked, because I knew it made good conversation to ask people about their successes.

"It was easy. There was a lot of paperwork, and steps that you had to go through, but the government was willing to loan the money. I don't know why other folks didn't want to take advantage of it, but the government loans were easy to get at the time... if you could show you had a plan."

"So, are you saying that it was easier to get started in your own independent business back then?"

"Pretty much. I set up a few accounts, applied for a loan, and the government gave me the money to set up the business."

"I don't think it's so easy anymore."

"Probably not. They got big chain outfits tying things up anyway."

"You still have the business?"

"No, no, it dried up a few years ago...mostly corporations running everything now."

We both sat for a moment without saying a word, then Leroy told me more of the story about the place where he lived, and once had a beer delivery business:

"There were a couple local churches. Some people didn't care to go to church, but a lot of people did, and the church would get together and help anyone that needed it, whether they went to church or not. There was a corner cafe where a lot of people would go hang out in the afternoon, and discuss things that were going on in the neighborhood, and everybody took care of each other. There wasn't a lot of crime. You could walk the streets at night. The whole place was clean, and a nice place to live."

He described a rather pleasant, and functional social interaction within a predominantly African-American community. After another pause, he continued his story, and I was a bit stunned by what Leroy said:

"Then this civil rights thing came along. Some of the guys who had been hanging around the corner cafe had run off to Denny's. The corner cafe suffered a loss of business, and people didn't gather to talk about the neighborhood anymore. The whole neighborhood began to suffer. People weren't going to the church, and nobody trying to help so much, while the problems that needed help were getting bigger every day. Fools were off at the racetrack, a bar or whorehouse, or some other place, and completely forgot about the neighborhood where they lived -- taking their business far away."

"So it was like people were looting their own homes by default?"

"Yeah, that civil rights thing came along, and the next thing you knew the whole neighborhood turned into a slum."

After a rather long pause, I said: "That was a very interesting story. I appreciate you telling me."

"Those were the days. I've got Social Security now. I'll be going back to Louisiana tomorrow."

"I hope you have a pleasant trip."

We sat for quite awhile without saying a word, just relaxing, and looking over the neighborhood. Finally, Leroy struggled to get up, and said; "Thanks for the tea and conversation," and headed back down the street toward Sapphire's place.

I talked to people in the cab about this 'civil rights thing'. One person who was familiar with my neighborhood pointed out that Frederick Douglas Plaza, which was about three blocks from where I lived, had been created in haste in order to be first to acknowledge an African-American holiday. So, it was supposed to be Frederick Douglas, but then it turned out to be Martin Luther King. Who picked Martin Luther King?

This begs the question: Who was in charge of this 'civil rights thing', anyway? So, you see, maybe there is a question, but nobody can answer it.

I didn't exactly understand what this all meant. It would be foolish to try to be against the Martin Luther King holiday, but it did seem that Martin Luther King was overly promoted – with special extra long signs, and in Berkeley they even put metal placards with a picture of Martin Luther King on every post along the street. Wouldn't 'King Street' be good enough? Huey Newton had a Ph.D., though we don't refer to him as "Dr." for some reason. Pharmacists, and some nurses, have Doctor Degrees, but when you go into a hospital you don't call your nurse 'doctor'. Usually, if a person has a doctor's degree in religious studies, as did Martin Luther King, they are simply called a 'preacher' or something. Any investigation of the facts would be too confusing, and emotionally charged, but I had to talk to people about it if no one else would, so…

Another response came from a young woman who was a student at California State University. I told her what Leroy had told me, and she responded, saying; "That old man didn't know what he was talking about. Some African-Americans just accepted the oppression that they suffered under segregation."

<>*You can't give equality to a group…*
Because everyone in the group will never be equal to each other <>

There had been a variety of arguments, like… *Histories of racism long ago in areas where long ago nobody even lived there.* Arguments of this caliber were generally ignored -- people wouldn't even point out the silliness, because they didn't want to get into the argument, be accused of being racist, or even waste their time on something nobody really believed.

Unreasonable arguments proliferated, and emerging generations would be confused, especially as they become more distanced from the facts, and the witnesses are silenced by the course of time.

One absurd, and often repeated argument in the civil rights era, was: If you were in a car wreck, and a black doctor ran to your aid – would you refuse treatment just because he was black? Obviously not, but if we were irritated by such a question... Did that mean we were racist? When do doctors run over to car wrecks, anyway? Does the black doctor have to be a man? Would we even be able to refuse an emergency rescue? How would we know that the black man running over to us was really a doctor? Should we assume that all black men running up on us are doctors? They might have to be, because all of the jobs that they used to have were eliminated... with the excuse that they were demeaning, or something. Mexicans would risk their lives to cross the border for whatever jobs were left -- not demeaning to them.

There were many arguments, some were based on facts, some only applied to isolated incidents, and some were totally ridiculous -- like building all sorts of evidence about a right that was secured for some specific group, and celebrating the fact, when that right had already been established many years ago. African Americans got the right to vote in 1968... But they already had the right to vote... Well, in some areas it was encumbered -- like the south... but Huey Long secured these rights to vote in Louisiana in the 1930s... Well, we'll celebrate the rights gained, anyway. A barrage of information from establishment media and other official channels drove the celebration, and the people didn't seem to notice that many rights were being taken away from everyone, including African-Americans, at the very same moment we were celebrating the rights.

The most powerful brainwashing ever to occur was the advent of color television, because when it was new -- the minds of people didn't differentiate it well from reality. Why did all this really happen? I sought out more opinions on this subject that people were so afraid to talk about, or even think about.

An old man who was about Leroy's age, a white man, told me that in the 1930s in the county where he lived... "There were very few black people, but my next door neighbor was a black man. He was a part of the neighborhood, and people didn't think of him according to his race -- he was just another farmer. There was an election for somebody to run the Water District, and my neighbor, a black man, ran for the office and was elected." The old man said that people these days believe that there was conflict back then, but there is more conflict now, because people are told that there is supposed to be conflict. "People are just doing what they are told," he said, "That's how it is nowadays, all bullshit."

I was getting other information – contrary to the advertised *Civil Rights* viewpoint -- a collection of things people were often reluctant to point out. For example: In the beginning of the cattle drives 25% of the cowboys were African-American, and; the world's largest retailer for years was Sear-Roebuck, and it should be noted that Roebuck was a black man. The list could go on. There wasn't always all this universal hate going on, or so much oppression as is said, but advertising would make it so. People were afraid to talk, and eventually the masses would believe in hate. I couldn't find the answer unless I found the right question to ask.

I interviewed an average of 20 people a night in the taxicab, and for a few days continued to sit at the bistro table in front of my apartment in the afternoon. On one occasion a black teenager sat down with me...

I asked him about his life, and after a while, he said; "You're a pretty cool guy, but the reason I set down here is that I thought you were the police when you called to me."

The police sitting at a bistro table on the sidewalk in a bad neighborhood sounds good, but it doesn't fit reality. "Well, I'm not the police." I made it clear.

The young man didn't sit long, but long enough to give me the opportunity to get his reaction to Leroy's story about the civil rights thing.

"What you mean? he asked aggressively, not waiting for an answer... "Back in the day I would have had to sit in the back of the bus. Black people couldn't vote. Are you saying that the civil rights thing wasn't real?!"

He left without either of us drawing any conclusions. There was nothing to argue about. Most people would agree that the idea of civil rights is a good thing. But there was something about Leroy's message that compelled my curiosity.

Putting together all I heard definitely presented a challenge. By the mid-eighties a black teenager believed that just before he was born black people had to ride in the back of the bus. In some places, just a few places, this was true. It wasn't true around here, not in California, and not in most places. If we're talking about down in someplace called 'The South', then we might want to think about that there are places way down yonder in that part of the country where they have strange rules -- I could get 10 years in prison if my wife gave me a blow job, for example. I personally would consider that to be rather extremely oppressive against me. Race might not be the real issue. In some respects it looked as if some candy coated poison had been passed off in the name of what most respectable people would believe to be a good thing. There were new laws, and in some cases it seemed that the public got blamed for something they didn't even have anything to do with. If there were oppressive laws, then those laws should have been removed.

The government was doing something wrong in some places, and they could stop it, contain it, or give it independence. Instead, the media driven government was pushing a general plan, and laws were made that affected what people do voluntarily. That doesn't make a lot of sense. Who was really causing what problem? People should be able to do whatever they want, and be able to be partitioned from things they don't want. If anything, a centralized power should be contained.

There is a good reason to partition things. Phone numbers are divided up so they are easy to manage, but the area code must come first. We can't think of people like that, so we end up not thinking about others at all. If we don't have the same interests we should at least have good communication.

Functionality may require a hierarchy of healthy boundaries. When there is too much data to unravel, the mode of looking away takes effect; just as we loathe to make eye contact with strangers on the streets of a crowded city. We start to filter out information, and not even see things, because there is just too much to process. Guys who are tremendously interested in girls, looking over the joys of an afternoon at the mall, filter out the fat chicks -- big women become invisible.

If you visit a high school, or anyplace where a diverse group of people congregate, you might observe Filipinos who appear to like to group together with other Filipinos; Blacks who seem to prefer the company of other Blacks, and other free associations that may be ethnically motivated. That's not necessarily racist – the racist construct includes hate, but freedom of association may be just a normal preference, and not be hateful at all. It used to be that people would establish neighborhoods in such a way – sometimes out of love for people they could call family. You had to want to be like family in some places -- A person could live anywhere they wanted, but often they had to gain acceptance into a neighborhood—like I did in a black neighborhood.

Laws were passed prohibiting people from controlling the demographics of their own neighborhood. Fear is used to manipulate people into agreeing with the government. Once fear is established, then laws are made to address fear... rather than provide any real solutions. One unfortunate consequence that countered whatever gains were being gifted was with the claim that black people could live in any neighborhood they wanted -- because now they didn't need to have their own neighborhood anymore, and could be required to pay the same high price as any other part of town. One of the things that came along with the benefits of civil rights was something called 'Gentrification'. Some of the neighbor's put up signs calling it racism, but just about everybody in the neighborhood seemed to be getting evicted, including me.

I was only paying $200 a month rent, and all of a sudden they could get $1000. Realtors and speculators were renaming the neighborhood 'Lower Haight', because 'Lower Fillmore' had negative connotations. Black people, or other people who gained acceptance into black neighborhoods could no longer enjoy bargain prices if somebody else thought that neighborhood was desirable. A new era of homelessness was about to emerge, and that occurrence would never get the emotional media push that 'race' issues had received. It was like a Trojan horse riding in bringing gifts to the oppressed minorities, and then opening up to take away what little they had. There was talk and talk and talk about rights that were being secured for the oppressed -- while the rug was being pulled out from under all of us, and everybody was having their rights diminished. The power of individuals and small groups were suppressed, and the power of government fortified. People couldn't control their own neighborhoods, and eventually wouldn't even talk to their neighbors anymore. So, now for sure we were going to need more police... so they'd say.

Another civil rights issue emerged... the rights of women. Equal pay for equal work was demanded, but it would never really happen.

What would happen is that society would change its functional requirement: That a man must have an income sufficient to support a family, or at least a spouse. Jobs shifted from manufacturing, to paper shuffling, and an economy developed where households required two incomes. Women, it had been traditionally assumed, didn't have to work, but if they did work – didn't get equal pay. That changed. Now they were going to have to work, and still not get equal pay. The option of paying people based on performance might have solved the problem, but the concept was not promoted ...as if an equitable solution wasn't even the real intention.

Developing media inundated the public to the degree of sensory overload and there was much too much to sort out -- even to acknowledge the confusion was too much to deal with, and people just filtered it out of their consciousness. There was growing confusion going on, and individuals couldn't talk about it; and because they didn't, people on the sidelines believed that the establishment claims were true.

The public assumed that because black people didn't vote somebody must have been stopping them. New sets of laws were supposed to solve this problem. Black people still didn't vote, because if you think about it; the kind of people who vote tend to believe in laws. We didn't need more laws, and we certainly didn't need more police. So what's to vote for? You get two bad choices when you go to vote -- who picks them?

Everyone should be treated with importance, but when there are too many people we are unfamiliar with we abandon refined perception.

The neighborhood used to be like family, but detached as we are becoming, we ignore the horrible circumstances of others.

We wouldn't let our sister eat out of a garbage can in the park, but now we're supposed to sit on a bench and enjoy the sunshine, and not even think about what's going on around us. We have become blind by going over our own limits. We don't recognize how to partition things to make them manageable. We make the mistake of leaving it up to the government -- our best attention devoured by electronic devices.

There were suspicious motives underlying the shifting culture. A broadcast of issues that could do nothing but create conflict had unleashed. The proliferation of advertising made people want what other people had. Culture had completely shifted -- from a people focused on what they do, to a people who only think about what they can get. We were supposed to want what big money and Corporations wanted us to want. We increasingly had to accept what corporations had to offer as they displaced small neighborhood shops. The neighborhood itself was fractured further as big money speculators were driving up the price of housing. Who was in charge? Not fictitious people sitting on a cloud, but an evil facsimile in our midst, and the media manipulators were now the new Voice of God. Therein lies the culprit—a 'fictitious person' otherwise known as a Corporation—which had grabbed the reins. The idea of 'culture' was ignored, as society was being railroaded deeper into a new culture, a variation of collectivism we might call *'Commercialism'*. We're supposed to worship money now, perhaps. Americans, while losing their freedom as individuals, had more freedom than ever - to go shopping.

Changes in society were disguised under the cover of race relations. What made race talk especially confusing is that the word "race" used to be synonymous with culture - but the definition mysteriously changed. At the end of WW II a famous speech referred to the American Race.

The word 'race' was synonymous with culture. When the definition shifted to refer only to physical appearance -- if there was an argument about something, we might have to concede that race doesn't really make any difference at all, at least by the new definition.

So, why even act like we can have a debate?

It's all about creating conflict, so we don't notice the wicked manipulation of our culture – ignoring the real threat because we are busy fighting each other. The people most concerned about race tend to be racists, and have fought to perpetuate hate. The population seemed to be embracing a whole bandwagon of shallow and errant reasoning. Culture, somehow surgically removed from the concept of race, was brushed aside almost entirely. Style of thinking, behavior, and aspirations -- the most significant components of a culture were ignored. Like being handed in empty glass that they could fill with anything they want. Superficiality overshadowed the innermost aspects of people. Race talk created confusion as the new Commercial Culture was ushered in. Should we just go shopping, and forget it?

Social issues were headed for a real train wreck. The physical and biological characteristics of people didn't concern me, and shouldn't, because the thing to be concerned about was what was happening to people's minds. I didn't care about 'race', but the issue of culture, overrun by a storm of racist nonsense, was begging me for attention, and I needed to take one more look.

I suspected that an analysis of culture might help us unravel the mystery of how functional social interaction occurs. I had been interested in understanding the differences in people for years, and had made a point to get to know people from 58 different countries. I sat for hours reviewing my notes on these encounters:

On one occasion, a couple from Sierra Leone had asked me to dinner. As their guests I was asked to select what we were to eat, and have it delivered. There was a Chinese restaurant that I liked because it had a special feast that included quite a collection of very distinctly different dishes. When the order arrived, the couple brought out a big bowl, poured all the dishes into it, and stirred them together. I was shocked, and thought it defeated the purpose.

The gentleman said; "This is how we do it at home," and I dug in with my fingers and smiled to conceal my dissatisfaction with the way the whole thing had transpired. This preference, I asked myself... Is it the resonance of a force that would favor collectivism? Is my dislike of the big bowl, or my appreciation of individual differences... is that a reflection of individualistic culture? Are these differences even things to be reckoned with?

It's pointless to try to force something that won't fit. We imagine that other people think like we do, because that's all our thinking will allow, but we should realize that we haven't even reached our own potential, so how can we evaluate the differences of others? We can't process so much information, and different people have different limits of the amount, and type of data they can comfortably process. Too much to think about disrupts our ability to think at all. Attorneys win cases by overloading the case with paperwork. In the society we live in today we are inundated with more than anyone can handle. How might this affect social interaction, and our own minds?

It seems that people who have extremely limited ability to process information may even get angry, or violent, for example; just by other people looking at them. Anyone might experience uneasiness if people look at them in an elevator, or dare to talk, but don't think it means they're supposed to fight. We fear social interaction, and want to hide.

We tend to shut out a lot of data, and even go into automatic pilot. Doing important things, and even dangerous tasks according to routines, and relying on automatic thinking—becoming hypnoids.

Different people have different cognitive limits, and there are some people who actually can only really deal with one idea at a time. The average person can look at a collection of things and identify how many things are there at a glance, as long as the number isn't above 5 or 6 -- but a few people can't even look at two items without counting. Different folks calculate differently. We need to acknowledge the position other people are at, and leave them alone if we can't find ourselves on the same page. When it's hard to sort things we group them, but in groups it's hard to recognize individual quality. So, we assume that a group is all equal, and will represent and support all who identify. Education can help, but everyone must travel on whatever path they're on, from wherever they are at a given time, and be allowed to make it on their own.

Sure, some African-Americans were oppressed, but so were Irish, Jews, and Native Americans, so what's the difference? The Okies were thoroughly hated when they arrived in the course of some of their migrations. Okies were white people (I guess), but I have trouble defining what white people really are, because there are so many alleged white groups that don't get along with each other. Black people were left out of the conflict between white groups, and because they could easily be identified at a distance, they were excluded more quickly. There is always likely to be resistance when demographics change. Black people were herded around the country to work in shipyards ...in areas where they were unfamiliar, and sometimes viewed as invaders. Then they were left hanging without a job– placed in housing projects worse than slums.

The government created a problem that only they could solve. African-Americans were deprived of working it out on their own like everyone else. They were not allowed to develop a society of their own choice — so maybe there would be race riots. But it had nothing to do with race… it was the government that caused the problem… with the proposal of more government as the sequential solution.

It's time for people to wake up, and fight to place the reigns of government back in the hands of the people – making the trek back toward Individual Sovereignty. We should hope to restrain the manipulative media, and require reparations for the harm it has done. Maybe it's about time for a race war after all – against an alien race of technological devices that are trying to make humans obsolete. Once we do away with the robots, we should be careful about the new rules we make for ourselves.

When it comes to what the rules are we should use restraint. When we stick our nose into other peoples business we look at their life according to how we are, or how we think, and should be reluctant to judge. Different cultures have different ways, which we should respect -- as well as be allowed to differentiate. Legislature should leave it to the people to police themselves.

People obey laws only because they agree with them, anyway. Some people imagine that other people can be forced to comply with what they themselves believe – even if they don't know why they believe what they do. If we don't agree, then we should agree not to agree, and leave it alone. Be careful about what rules you think you want for others, because true justice may give us too much to think about.

There are a number of ways we cope with the processing a mass of information, more things to think about, more people to deal with, etc.

We may use a system of hierarchy, stratification, or other things to keep a semblance of order, or we will look for help from outside ourselves to fix the problem for us.

We may think we need more rules, and even inappropriately demand it. When overloaded, our engagement with processing some information may fade to a degree of blindness.

We find methods to organize our needs, filter out whatever doesn't strongly demand our attention, look to authorities, or use other devices, which may make us feel that everything is OK, when it is not.

In order to relate to things we aren't particularly interested in we also utilize labeling (racist, convict, crazy, etc.) to try to identify our world, and make it simple. Yet, reliance on labels actually complicates problems, encumbers communication, and can actually block any kind of improvement we may hope to see. Labels represent an attempt to try to partition things, but outside of a functional context it does no good. We may easily agree with things that are distanced from us, and not realize that they may come back to haunt us.

Looking at the parts of the puzzle I was trying to put together revealed a dire emergency — up ahead, on the route that social interaction was taking was certain doom. Real change must occur before it's too late to treat the condition.

The most important step in solving a problem is to identify what the problem really is, but racist accusations can sidetrack the issue to a question that can't be answered. To label a person a 'convict' may make it impossible for him to ever be recognized as a good citizen — or even get a job. We cling to absurd constructs involving terrorists, predators, mafias, and other descriptions of evil – while ignoring that our air and water are being poisoned. To secure our identity, and try to make sense of the world we may try to label everything. People try to label their neighborhoods with some lofty name suggested by the Realtor, and ignore that it's not even really a neighborhood at all — they don't even know their neighbors.

Slogans may also have the same impact as labels. As people try to partition improperly, and categorize their world in a realm of fantasy. As this all goes on, you may cling to a belief in some label out of fear that if you let go that the floodgate of chaos will open. You'll cherish beliefs in authorities that know everything, and can solve any problem—excusing yourself from responsibility. When it's time for action... You'll wish you could just push a button, or take a pill to make things happen. You'll ignore entirely that you are falling deeper into an abyss.

I suddenly realized something... a purpose that labeling, and grouping things serve. Just like when a half million people died in the Civil War for peoples rights, and a greater day for democracy was enjoyed for a little while... but then the laws designed to protect the people became something used to empower corporations. Corporations became a powerful menace, and the rights of people systematically diminished through their advances. A group, called a Corporation, had usurped the power of Natural Persons. If there was something suspicious about the talk concerning the Civil Rights Movement in more recent times – all you have to do is imagine who would benefit if everybody were thought of as part of a group rather than as individuals. If everyone was encouraged to focus on groups -- which group would win? The group that would come out on top is called a corporation, and as a 'fictitious person' the only 'individual' left that counts. A shrewd trick to usher in the collective culture of Commercialism with the corporate controlled media moving us along at their whim.

By force of advertising promotions, people have been manipulated to take no pride in what they do, and just focus what they can get -- they will fuss, they will steal, they will go shopping, but the brainwashed masses won't do anything to sustain quality in our society. Under the power of corporate influence -- many people resign to the idea of participating in a consumer craze to build a mountain of junk.

Corporations need to be dismantled, and the negative influence on culture reversed – but how could such a proposal even be presented?

So much has been embedded in emotionally charged cognitive constructs since the public first placed its eyes on a color television. *Race* talk, which began at the pinnacle of mass media cognitive impact, would later move over to place *safety talk* at the forefront of manipulative media. The question of who is in charge of it all gets lost in the shuffle -- they'd even say; *'you are, the public is'* -- as the overbearing procession of bullshit further embellishes the throne of the new King -- the Corporation.

Part of the problem with any argument could be in the arena it is held in, so I had to find a new way to look at the issues. The way things were presented seemed to be rigged to have no solution. The real problem hadn't been identified, or portions of it not disclosed. Race, religion, and politics were important issues that couldn't be discussed. A moderator was missing, or something else was wrong. How the concept of culture had been altered – therein may lay a clue.

In analysis of culture, I was more interested in the spirit of it than its artifacts. There is a tendency to want to look at culture as static -- something to anchor to -- but culture is always in flux, so I considered the moving force, and the direction it was going to be the most important point to attend to. It appeared to me that the continuum between individualism and collectivism seemed to be the most dominant and important factor.

I wanted to chart a map for cultural analysis, and use numbers to avoid the bias attached to names, so... On a scale going from –5 to +5 I placed extreme Collectivism at +5 and extreme Individualism at -5. I postulated that to go beyond these outermost extremes would not be possible. Attempting to go beyond 5 would trigger an impulse to move to the opposite side of the spectrum.

The furthest extent of individualism would result in chaos. The furthest extreme of collectivism would also initialize a destructive process. There could possibly be a balance to the formula made by contributing factors, and I wanted to explore this idea.

I made a list of contrary factors in two columns headlined by Individualism vs. Collectivism. Below Individualism I entered Creativity, and on the other end of the continuum under Collectivism placed Conformity -- listing counterparts on opposite ends of a continuum. Then added: Nature vs. Artifice, Freedom vs. Slavery, Liberty vs. Safety, Industry vs. Finance, Regionalism vs. Globalism, etc. I labeled the left column "A", and the right column "Z" instead of Individualism and Collectivism respectively. Generic labels reduced the threat of variants in the definition of words. I had to allow for variants mathematically instead of by definition.

I came up with factors to add to the list in a variety of ways. One of many directions I took was with the most ancient roots of popular thought, and dug into The Rig Veda, which is believed by many to be the first literature of Western Civilization, and carries a theme of conflict between an Individualistic culture that maintains a reverence for Nature, and an opponent who had an apparent reverence for statuary, jewelry, and other man-made creations. The literature includes many incantations to the Gods of Nature, calling for aid to defeat an enemy--lest Nature itself be destroyed.

The purveyors of this literature had such aversion to man-made devices that they even considered the art of writing to be an abomination, and passed the message for thousands of years strictly through memorization.

I read the entire text – 10,000 stanzas of peculiar poetry, and then compared it with other writings.

I looked at even the most secret texts of various religions, the philosophies of Aristotle and others, or anything that could provide a clue about the foundations, and movements, of popular thought. Every thought came from somewhere -- from a progression of other thoughts passed along through time. I imagined that analyzing these things would help identify factors to be placed on the continuum.

Consider how representation of various factors might be approached. Some of them, like Individualism vs. Collectivism, may encompass the entire range of the continuum, or 11 digits (including zero), and the points in between. Other factors might be one sided, or have a range of only 5 or 6...like Honor. We can say Honor vs. Law by one interpretation, but there are different definitions of Honor in different cultures. Perhaps subscripts may have to be added to some factors, like 1, 2, and 3 for different interpretations. One idea of Honor might have a range, for example, that rests from –4 to +1, and another may be found only on the plus side.

Whether one sided, or full spectrum, I considered a lot of factors for inclusion; even Love vs. Hate. I also considered that some factors might need to have weighted values in order to calculate within a matrix accurately. All of the factors, measured against each other could determine compatibility, or predict the movement of culture, or zeitgeist -- as well as other applications.

I speculated, after compiling much data, that this information could have several uses: To identify a cultural locus by a number, and thus avoid the stigma of other labels; to enhance style of communication effectiveness, to establish a range within which you might want to position yourself, or to predict the outcome of social organizations... There appeared to be many uses.

Zeitgeist Scale

```
_____A_____...._____Z_____
-5 .... -4 .... -3... -2 ... -1.... 0 ... +1 ... +2... +3... +4... +5
```

Individualism .... Collectivism

Nature .... Artifice

Freedom   ... ... Slavery

Liberty .... Safety

Industry .... Finance

Analytical ... . Reactive

Treatment .... Punishment

Performance ... ... Possessions

Ability .... Endorsement

Stratification ....Universality

Empathy .... Detachment

Segregation ... ... Integration

Honor....................……Law

After compiling 37 factors and their counterparts, with subgroups in 9 factors, as well as a list of modulators, I constructed a scale for the analysis of something I called *Zeitgeist* (a German word that doesn't have an English equivalent). 'Zeitgeist' was an unfamiliar word to most people at the time that I used it to define my analytical method. The word has since made its way into several languages, and is generally defined as 'spirit of the time', and refers to intellectual and cultural climate of an era. In the German language, taken literally from 'zeit' (or time); and 'geist' (or spirit) it initially had a much deeper meaning; 'zeitgeist' is not just a time, but also a movement, because time is always in motion. A way it had been presented in the past was that time is taken as having material meaning and having substance; the ghost that rides above it provides direction. As I see it, Zeitgeist refers to a worldview on a social cultural progression. To map the conditions of culture is one thing, but to analyze the magnitude and direction of the forces of culture may be more useful. The word 'Zeitgeist', the way I understood it, was the most effective word to describe what I was trying to analyze --*The nature of the moving force of culture* is how I define *Zeitgeist*.

As the data came together it started to reveal a fantastic formula. Then the formula found a snag -- in Japan. According to the factors on the scale, the cultural forces of Japan were Individualistic, however, the Japanese are widely regarded as a collective culture. Japanese culture very clearly appeared to be on the "A" side, yet people insist that it is a Collective Culture. The one factor that skewed the analysis was Conformity—a powerful thing that must be, I thought, but how could this one component contaminate a culture to change it's appearance entirely, and what does this all mean?

To answer this question I took out my best research tool, the taxicab.

While in the taxi I tried to hang around Japan Town, and frequented places that were popular amongst Japanese tourists. I looked for people of Japanese descent to talk to, and read whatever I could find that seemed to pertain to Japanese people.

I even considered learning the Japanese language, but it appeared that I wouldn't be easily understood-- all I really learned how to say was I don't speak Japanese, in Japanese, and didn't do that very well. It became a way of joking with Japanese people, and they thought it hilarious.

In regard to my question about individuality or collectivism I found articles about Japanese business that were quite interesting. The claim was that Japanese businesses operate more efficiently because individuals are treated more importantly, and there is a greater deal of enthusiasm and diligence applied to their work.

In contrast, if we look at the roots of American big business to compare... it appears that there was an effort to move toward collective mechanisms to a degree that the only individuals that mattered were the bosses. In this scenario, because of the abuse of workers, (who were sometimes treated even worse than slaves), it is understandable that workers established unions (which ironically seemed to evolve to advocate collectivism). Collectivism used to fight collectivism as if it was the only system that existed. It would be erroneous within a true Individualistic culture to form a collective. With a similar appearance, but having a different nature, a *cooperative* is more suited to Individualism. How could this apply to my question about the Japanese anomaly? How could it relate to the differences in American business?

I had a lot of questions, and the answer seemed to lie between the balance of Individualism and Collectivism.

The interaction between individualism and collectivism operates on a cycle, because a collective cannot exist without the product of individuals.

Collective efforts have some usefulness, but shouldn't be developed to the point where they are considered individuals in themselves, and the mob ruler is all that matters – as it is with corporations. Individuals can easily be swallowed by a mob, but then the mob will suffer once they are left in wanting of individual initiative.

Human beings, it should be noted, are individuals. Any culture built by humans should not have a resemblance to a culture of insects, like termites and bees — which aren't individualistic at all. Collectives may be called for in the hope of managing chaos, or providing balance, but should have clearly defined limits. Instead of bringing about unions in an attempt to suppress the abuse by industry, the very existence of such errant businesses should not be condoned -- organizations of more than 20 people should be employee owned. When the mob comes to the aid of individuals, the individual can easily be destroyed for the sake of the mob. If enslaved by a monster we might easily accept any efforts for relief, and let the monster live to devise its methods of oppressing us ...unwittingly perpetuating our call for a savior that will never solve our problem. How did the Japanese manage?

To analyze the condition of Individuality we can look at the appeal of authority. In conversations with Japanese people I was surprised to learn about the absence of police. Not long ago, at least in some provinces, there were no police at all, so I was told. I also noticed a difference, in that younger people insisted that the Japanese were a collective culture, but older people sometimes emphasize that it was a culture based on individualism. One woman I met, born in Japan, but now living in America, expressed a great deal of irritation with Japanese culture -- because there was just too much conformity. She told me that in Japanese history there were no police, and people were divided into groups of five in order to police themselves.

I was excited about the potential correlation with cognitive limits, and got so caught up in the woman's wild dissertation against conformity — I stuttered, and the woman had already jumped out of the cab before I could ask some questions. Perhaps it was five households that would group together to police themselves – I don't know.

Perhaps the problem arose when these people, long ago, started reporting to authorities. If things seemed difficult -- did they pass the buck, and suffer the consequences of giving up personal control? The factor of conformity could add stress, and have particular effects upon Zeitgeist, but to also add a component of authority could push it to the outer limits. Could it be that a rather advanced individualistic culture could be smothered and strangled by two simple factors in conflict? What would happen if small support groups formed in Japan that encouraged seeking the limits of creativity instead of conformity?

Long ago, no doubt to address some threat of chaos, an adjustment added into the system which evolved over years into blind conformity, and rituals related to conformity, to a degree far removed from just bringing culture into balance.

It seems that the controls of society work best if they are closer to the hand of the individual, which, I concluded, is where we must focus, because; if we ignore the needs of an individual, eventually our own needs as individuals shall be ignored. Defense of Individuality is vital, because it is too easy to get run over by a mob.

Individual Sovereignty must be secured first. The next step from the individual is a couple, and I tried to map it:

The Individual, a Natural Person, should be the principal focus; a couple could mean an argument when individuality is violated; three could mean a conspiracy; four might be called an organization, and five people opens the door to a need to split, or have some rules. Larger numbers have greater difficulty in serving individuals fairly, and *six* is the threshold of chaos.

Seven calls for a leader — but with a leader there is the risk that the potential power of seven individuals can become just one, the leader — thus usurping Individuality entirely. I wanted to find a way to write it all down.

Then I lost my job, and was about to lose my license. I suddenly had a lot of time to write, and compile lots of information. I hadn't planned it like that. I hadn't received a ticket in 6 years, but suddenly got 4 of them within two weeks. I don't know how the cab company found out, but they held me out of service until I got the tickets cleared up. Evidently, I was driving while black – of course not, but there had been issues in the media about the way taxi drivers often drive. They do it to get from one place to another, but that's beside the point. I got a ticket for going 58 in a 55 — which is legal I thought, and the officer didn't answer when I asked him why he gave me a speeding ticket when other people were passing me. He said nothing, and just gave me the ticket and walked away. Another officer argued with me when he gave me a ticket for running a red light -- when I was stopped at the light in question -- saying; "It looks to me that you are at least 6 inches over the line." Another ticket was received when I drove by a popcorn stand, and honked at a girl I knew there — cops, on foot, acting like jock heros, ran to catch me at a stoplight, claiming that I was honking at pedestrians to chase them out of the way. The tickets were ridiculous, but I had to wait out the court dates to clear them up. It was a serious problem, because in California if you get 4 tickets within a year you lose your license.

I stayed home, for fear of getting that final ticket, and put together about 40 pages of ideas considering a long list of factors that could be included in the *Zeitgeist Scale*.

It may be that some factors may have a range of seven according to a particular definition of the factor, and for example; rest at four on one side of the scale and two on the other.

In this way, if a numeric value could be applied to an attribute that could be clearly defined, and by identifying its position on one side of the scale, we might be able to determine the optimum resting point on the other side.

Other methods were attempted in order to establish appropriate values. The sum of the numeric value of all factors considered; divided by the number of factors, and then divided by six in order to determine the range and placement on a scale -- tendencies for direction of movement, extraneous strata to consider when particular points in the scale were reached, and countless other speculations engaged me.

I also put together as many pages about variations in cognitive limits: To help manage our finances we might have a spouse, a banker, and an accountant -- three people, OK-- but to have six people involved in our personal finances might be getting to be too many. You might let 6 people hold the keys to your car; including yourself, your wife, three kids, and your mother-in-law—maybe too many. You wouldn't let 20 people hold the keys to your car, but you might ask 20 people to keep an eye on it because someone was messing with it. You wouldn't ask 150 people to watch your car, because not so many people are likely to care, and they might not even know what your car looks like—so, you might as well ask the person messing with your car to keep an eye on it. Among other speculations I considered the amount of stress compared to the number of miles in a commute, or the number of times a person had to fly far from home on business. A group of up to around 6 might be called *Symbiotic*, or Bonded. A group size of up to around 22 might be called *Sympathetic*.

The hypothesis determined a limit beyond where Chaos would occur according to various applications, e.g:

Personal effort = 6,
Sympathetic effort = 22,
Participatory effort = 39,
Community effort = 152.

I wrote 80 pages about strains of influence that passed through world history, and many more pages about proper partitions, improper labeling, over-reliance upon authority, the threat of excesses in automatic thinking, the power of social networks, the responsibility of individuals, and the importance of Individual Sovereignty. Over 300 pages in all, and to survey people about it I no longer had the taxi as a research tool, so I put together an essay that some friends circulated on the street. For this, I was accused of being another Charles Manson or something, of course. I never can believe how simple-minded people can be with their labeling, and wouldn't think that anyone would take some paranoid accusation seriously, but what happened next was really over the top.

Federal Agents ransacked my apartment. I would never know why, but the ATF and FBI raided my home. Could it be that the essay that I distributed might have been construed to be a call to overthrow the government? There had been a growing movement in the mid-1980s to overthrow the government, which climaxed in 1986 with the first sedition trial in American history. I didn't have any part of it, but a lot of people didn't even notice it was happening, and there's so much that too many people don't notice. I noticed too much. My philosophy shouldn't justify a Federal raid. Could it have been because of what a former roommate had done? I didn't think so. They confiscated a stack of books, a knife collection, cases of gift items that I thought of selling to make a living, and an American flag... None of these things were illegal.

If you think it's OK for authorities to come into my home, loot the place, and tear it up so bad as to make it unlivable; then it has to be OK for them to do it to you -- it could happen, and it's not OK. I called the police to ask them what was going on. They wouldn't tell me anything over the phone, and just invited me to come down and we could talk about it. I called my attorney, and waited for him to find out something.

My attorney got back to me, and told me not to go to the police. He couldn't find out any details, except that I was on a 'dangerous persons list', and he'd never heard of that, but it would cost me $500,000 to get out of jail if I went down to talk to the police. He insisted that I just keep a low profile, and wait until the police come to get me -- they might not even look, he suggested. This was too strange, but I thought about a couple of recent incidents in which people's homes were raided, but the media referred to their homes as compounds, and all of the inhabitants in these compounds died -- the evidence destroyed by fire. The fire, coincidentally, was always because of a kerosene lantern. So, to my alarm, when I broke into my boarded-up apartment after the raid -- the place torn shreds, and my property stolen -- I noticed a kerosene lantern sitting in the middle of my dining room table, and; I didn't own a kerosene lantern. I'd take my attorneys advice. I was on the run, but I had to move anyway. I lost all the writing that I had done, but I had other problems to worry about.

It took more than two years before I was apprehended. While standing on a street corner with a group of friends, the police ran up, insisting that they saw us doing something with some drugs. They insisted that they saw, implying that they had probable cause allowing them to search us all, but didn't see well enough that they could clarify who or what they really saw. After threatening to strip search us all, they proceeded to run ID checks-- something they can do without cause.

If you think it's OK for the police to do this, then perhaps you spend most of your time at home watching TV, and aren't so much in a position for the police to do it to you. In any event, you shouldn't condone them doing it to anyone.

Don't assume, as hard as it is to depart from the assumption, that the authorities are doing everything right. It isn't right, but at least the abuse on the street corner by police ended for the other parties when they came to me. They quickly chased everyone else away, and turned to ask me:

"Are you armed and dangerous?"

" No," I replied.

"Well, we have a warrant for your arrest."

I figured this was it, and asked them what it was about. They said they didn't know. I sat in a holding cell at the police station for several hours before an officer returned to say that they couldn't find any paperwork on any charges against me, and it appeared that all I had to do was pay a traffic ticket for San Francisco, and I would be released. They didn't care about traffic violations in other jurisdictions, and that's all I had against me.

"Will you take a check?" I asked, enthusiastically. They did. I was free.

All I had to do was clear my other tickets, and then I could get my life back on track, because the only work I seemed to be able to get required me to have a driver's license. It's not so easy, because if you say you can't afford to pay $50, their response may be: "Well then, pay $300." When people are down and out, this strange system that we allow to perpetuate beats people down further. I had to go to two different courts for the three other tickets that I got in those dreadful two weeks, but I also had four other tickets in four separate counties for registration violation.

At one point, I was driving around looking for a job, and didn't realize that it was a moving violation to have an expired registration--until the fourth officer explained it to me. As the ticket pile grew taller... seven tickets had failure to appear violations attached to all of them, and there were failure to pay fine violations, as well as a couple of other added penalties.

The total amount of fines was over $6,000, and my license would remain suspended even if I had the means to pay.

I spent the next six months going to courts. To satisfy some of the offenses, I completed 360 hours of community service at a homeless shelter -- where I also got to eat. I brought evidence of this, along with all the paperwork from various courts to my next court appearance, and asked the judge to look at it. The judge dismissed the charges, saying that I had been through enough, and I had plenty more to go through. I had been reading law books in the quest for reasoning with the traffic courts, but was only saved by mercy.

Back in 1968, the rights of citizens in traffic court were severely compromised. It used to be that the public didn't just have to answer to a judge; the judge also had to answer to the public. There was no defense in traffic court anymore. In one of the courts I went to — in a desperate attempt to exercise some kind of rights -- I used a technicality of challenging the judge, and was lucky enough to be sent to an alternate who didn't have a show to put on, and didn't like the judge that I had cited as prejudiced (to be excused without the requirement of an explanation). That got dismissed too. The last stop was the treacherous San Mateo County court. I had gone to the court three times, and the best I could come up with was that they wanted $400. With just that holding me back from getting my license, and possibly a job, I was able to borrow the money. Some people aren't so lucky.

I finally got my license back, but there was no way that I was going to get a job, because when I got the print out from the DMV there were 27 entries on my driving record. The only job I was able to get that didn't require driving was as a part-time piano teacher. I didn't know how to play the piano, but one day at the mall I overheard an argument at a piano store about their teachers.

In a friendly manner I introduced myself, and the manager, so enraged by his piano teachers, hired me on the spot without checking my qualifications. I taught beginning students, so I was able to fake it for several months. Unfortunately, it was only four hours a week, and my life savings grew painfully slow -- to just over $300, yet I owed $400.

Always looking for another opportunity, and obviously needing something, I obtained a real estate license by going to the library, reading a book, and taking the test just before the law was changed. The law would change with a lot of added red tape -- to establish some imaginary benefit through a more rigid bureaucratic process. I got the real estate license, but it wasn't going to do me any good -- it takes ages before you get paid when you first start.

Between the piano store and the real Estate office I spent a lot of time being broke. The only way I could come up with any cash on a daily basis was by giving people rides in exchange for gas money. I wanted to drive, but this wasn't what I had in mind, and I wished I could drive to another planet. I had never been out of the Bay Area except to Seattle for a couple of years, but I was anxious to live anywhere, as long as it wasn't in my car anymore. Feeling hopeless, I just wanted to escape, and started driving east toward the Altamont pass.

I drove East to a realm I'd never ventured, driving as if running away from life itself. I was wearing a suit and tie as if I had some important business to attend, but I didn't even have a specific destination in mind, or a plan of any kind -- I just kept driving, and thinking about driving. I saw a couple of accidents along the way, but in my opinion there is no such thing as an accident -- it's always negligence. For me it's true, because I'm a professional.

I often thought about other people driving, and what they were thinking, and came to the conclusion that they were not thinking at all. Something should be done, because this scares me, but if they made a law against daydreaming while driving... oh, what a wonderful example about the ineffectiveness of law that would be. Of course, when an officer sees the consequences of an automobile accident -- mangled dead bodies strewn across the road-- he is motivated to do something to prevent it. But giving tickets doesn't make people better drivers-- it only produces revenue under the rationale of somehow forcing safer driving. For some things automatic thinking is necessary, and driving engages automatic thinking to an extreme. The part of the brain that operates automatic processes doesn't acknowledge the meaning of a traffic ticket. If it could, it would be equivalent to imposing severe mental illness. It's as if upon viewing an alleged traffic violation an officer issues a ticket to your brother -- who isn't even there. The brother might beat you up, but that might not do any good, and you could be just fighting all the time -- the action has an inherent harm. Well, if daydreaming was recognized as a violation, officials might realize that it is something they can't enforce. Daydreaming is a significant factor in automobile collisions, but being unenforceable it doesn't fit the game. I wish they'd quit playing. We don't need all this CHP – they are just tax collectors with guns. My mind raced with thoughts, but it wasn't like an ordinary daydream, because I was so angry.

Without falling too deep into my own thoughts, continuously analyzing and planning strategies as I rolled along on the freeway, I reviewed the object of my departure. I tried to ignore it, but the ATF, the ticket fiasco, and all of the other fixtures in our world that seemed to abandon reasoning and had interfered with my life-- the ordeal that had pounded my thoughts for so long. It remained like a dark cloud over my mind.

I wanted to leave it all behind, and just kept driving with no place to go except *away*. Yes, like everyone else, I was guilty of pondering something other than performing the most dangerous act that normal people do-- riding in a ton of steel and plastic at a high rate of speed. Angry, frustrated, I just kept driving on a path to nowhere, as my mind wandered.

I was angry at what the government was doing, and how the police had dealt me a lousy hand. Seeing lights flash on the side of the road drove me deeper into a rage... thinking about police services. I remembered a police officer telling me: "I'm going to put handcuffs on you for your safety." For my safety? Perhaps it's that police usually don't shoot people who are handcuffed. Police certainly do shoot people unnecessarily, and the standard procedures that allow it should be eradicated. To kill people based on a very remote, or totally imaginary threat is unconscionable, but police shoot people when there is clearly no threat at all. I remembered the story of a 16-year-old boy in Pacheco who was shot in the back by police because he ran when they wanted to ask him a question -- the boy had never committed a crime. I wondered what that boy was like. Then there was the advertising executive who the police shot multiple times, allegedly because the gentleman threatened the safety of an officer by trying to drive away in his $90,000 car. Was he a criminal? What really happened? A technicality that allowed the police to use deadly force without the inconvenience of public scrutiny -- and it could have been you. It happens all the time, and we ignore it, assuming all is proper. At a theater down the street from where the respectable businessman was shot, a teenager with a Boy Scout knife was shot over 20 times, and frankly, I personally wouldn't consider the little knife to be such a threat as to justify that action. Supposedly, the public excuses these actions because the police place themselves "in harms way" on a daily basis. No they don't!

I'm a taxi driver, and that's much more dangerous than police work. For the police to be trigger-happy bastards doesn't make them any safer, and certainly doesn't add to the safety of the public (in the name of Public Safety). They are cowards, because I know for certain that I could subdue a retard with a Boy Scout knife without having a gun at all in my possession. I know that the police put up with a lot of nonsense, and might be driven to shoot people out of convenience, or the enticement of a three-day paid administrative leave. I witnessed these things, and heard many stories, so I can't ignore it so easily. An 18-year-old kid who hired my cab at the hospital, told me about a domestic dispute at his home: His mom had called the police because of an argument. The police came, shot his dog in the yard, and then shot his dad through a window. In view of these revelations, and many more that I could tell you about, I might suggest not calling the police at all, ever. Can we call them to leave us alone? The fact is that the majority of calls to police are not real emergencies anyway, and we truly need to have someone else to call when we need help. We could get by with 10% of the police services that are forced on us – and police get paid way too much, so we could save a lot of money. We don't need so much expensive government – It's not that useful. I kept driving as if escaping, but my thoughts tortured me. I couldn't stop thinking about it, and wondered if I was going crazy... My irritation with government agencies mixed with crazy in my fatigued mind.

A woman who was supposedly known to be mentally ill called police, but these agencies with all of their power and privilege don't communicate effectively – so they didn't know she was crazy. She called the police because her son was angry, and she wanted the police to come to calm him down.

It's normal for teenagers to have their fits – but do we call the police for that?

She had previously informed the courts in a letter, when her son was arrested on a truancy violation, that she couldn't handle her son, and asked that he be placed in foster care because of her mental condition. The courts ignored this, sent the boy home, and his mother almost right away called the police. The boy was angry about something, and his mother exaggerated what the problem was -- but just wanted the police to help. The police came and shot the boy in the head. The claim was that he had a gun, but then the claim was that he didn't have a gun, and it was said that they shot the boy just because he wasn't cooperating. People near the scene said that the police were especially rude, and the mother was forcefully taken a block away while police cordoned off the whole area just because the boy refused to come out of his room. Everybody just wanted the police to go away. When no one could see, the police shot the boy in the top side of the head while he was less than 8 ft. from a wall, and blood and brains that blasted from the back of his skull formed a pattern centered at 1 ft. and one quarter inches from the ground. The boy was about 5 ft. 8 in. tall, so, from these measurements that I took myself, it appears that he must've been on his knees or something when they shot him in the head. I knew the boy, and he wouldn't come outside with the police there – I'm sure. His mother said they pulled him out the window – I don't know, but that could explain the blood splatter. Police reports aren't available to the public, but there should be more than public scrutiny — there should be outrage. We should quit assuming that these things are proper, and quit allowing ourselves to think we don't care. You should make sure it doesn't happen to anybody, because if it happens to anybody it could happen to you; and when it happens to you nobody will care.

Stuck in a rage, I just kept driving as if running away...
with no place to fun. Society had been changing, and evolving
into something grotesque. A historical perspective may be
important, especially if we analyze it on a continuum of
popular cognitive constructs. But there were tricks, like all of
the rights that everyone lost in 1968: The attack on individual
rights; the right to bear arms, the right to be represented by an
attorney or have a jury trial for all court appearances; the right
to elect even nominal public officials, freedom of religion,
freedom of association, and other rights all seemed to have
mysteriously vanished -- without protest, or even any
memory of them. It's a clue to the power of brainwashing, but
we never want to admit it once we have become a victim.
Sure, institutional segregation ended in 1968 -- but in just a
few years the overpaid guards in the California State prison
system would grow to exceed the entire statewide prison
population of 1968, and most of those prisoners would be
African-Americans. Isn't this an especially horrible type of
segregation? Where is all this equality that was talked about?
How would benefits to the group be dispersed? The
administrators themselves will become the beneficiaries, and
they will engage in wastefulness – just like corporations do to
enrich a few. For many, the only benefit is the illusion – like
buying a lottery ticket, and dreaming.

Where was our society going? My head was spinning,
and not knowing where I was going, I just kept driving as if to
get away from it all. From my frame of mind, we were all on
an express train to disaster. Chaos is at hand.

Up ahead the sign said Stockton. I wanted to exit the
freeway, and pretend that I was entering a whole new world.
If there was anything to do for others, I had to deal with my
own immediate problems first, and a new place might put my
mind at ease to make a plan. I exited the freeway to look for a
place to relax.

I sat down at a café to look at the local newspaper, and had a final thought as if to get a long awaited answer: We can't butt heads to make amends, we can't argue against a sea of lies, we can't turn the clock back. My ambition would not be to turn the clock back, but to break the clock. I desperately scanned the newspaper, as if it would have an answer...

An ad in the paper lead me to a local Realtors office where I met Paul McCormick, and as I sat down with him my anxiety seemed to wane. He had a rather imposing birthmark covering half of his face — otherwise he'd look like Elvis Presley. I had to have an explanation in order to adjust to his appearance, and he also told me about how he was run over by a truck when he was 18, and continued to have trouble walking ever since. Wondering what life was like for him took my mind off of my own problems. This man had a hard life, and would understand, I thought, and would never cheat me. He seemed like a kind, very innocent man, sitting alone in his real estate office -- always alone, and by himself. Nothing in the world seemed to really matter, so even if it would amount to nothing I offered to place my real estate license with him. After the formalities were over, I said:

"Well, you finally got an agent to help out around here."

"Yes, I'm very glad you came to Stockton," said Paul.

"I didn't know I was coming here. I live in my car, and sometimes I drive it places."

Paul Laughed.

"I guess the best place for a homeless person to be is in a real estate office," I said.

"How much money have you got?" Paul asked.

"About $300."

Paul laughed, and continued to laugh while he muttered something about pulling a rabbit out of a hat.

I was looking over some real estate information, and got the impression that Stockton might have the lowest prices in the State.

Paul didn't seem to be able to stop laughing as he got on the phone. His laughing turned to a stutter, which was normal for him, as he started talking to someone:

"I've got an investor from the Bay Area sitting in my office, and he may be interested in that house that you've wanted to sell for the longest time; provided you carry the paper, and with a six months lease option so the investor can get a feel of the market before he jumps in."

I couldn't believe what I was hearing, but then Paul got off the phone, and said;

"You wanna go look at a House?"

"Uh, yeah," I said, a bit confused.

We went to look at a small two-bedroom house that a lot of people might refer to as a shack -- situated on a dirt road on the edge of town. It was understandable that the seller had it on the market for a couple years without a single offer, and it was in a condition below the level that any bank would be willing to lend on.

"OK Paul, I'll put my whole $300 on this, and if the seller will except that, then I'll take care of the cleanup, because there's a lot needed, and then I'll start giving him $500 a month on the first."

Paul smiled; "That might work, because $500 is more than he'd ever get for rent, and he hasn't been able to sell it. I'm not worried about the commission, because I don't make any money anyway."

We went back to the office and wrote up a contract, Paul still laughing. The buyer accepted the offer, and I ended my homelessness by buying a house with only $300 in my pocket. The next question would be how I was going to make the payments, because if I made any money in real estate it wouldn't be for months.

Amazed at what had just happened, I quickly drove back to The City and started searching the streets. I spotted a girl that I knew -- crouched in a doorway. I could read what was going on in her life, and asked her;

"Have you had enough? You want to make a change and get out of this mess?"

"I'm sick of this," she said, "but I've been clean for two days."

"If you want to stay clean I got you a room out of town for $250 a month."

"$250, that's cheap!"

"It's in Stockton."

"Good, away from here, and I really do want to straighten up."

"Yeah, well, you know what I've been through, and finally I got a place, so I can't fool around about it. I can help you, but I need the $250 without a problem."

"I appreciate it, and I'll come through."

"Have you got $250?"

"No."

"How soon can you get it?"

"An hour, or two hours…I don't know."

"How about by midnight?"

"Fo' sure."

"Ok then, be here at midnight with $250 and I'll take you with me. We can clean up this house and you can pick what room you want, and then we can find another girl who wants a way out of this trap, and she can rent the other room."

"Way cool."

"Yeah, but I need $500 on the first every month, so I've got to find another renter."

"Don't worry, that's easy," she said, "and I've got a regular that will come to Stockton once a week to pay my rent."

The house had a full basement, which was just a cement basement, but luxurious to me after suffering with homelessness for so long.

To make the payments I rented the two rooms to prostitutes who felt that the merry-go-round they were on was getting ugly, and wanted a chance for change.

The rent was so cheap, compared to the $70 a night hotel rooms they were used to, that just hanging on to a couple of their regulars could help them stay above water until they found a real job—speaking optimistically.

At least I had a way to pay the rent at the moment, and could enjoy my new basement living until I found a real job. Being a real estate agent wasn't reliable, even Paul, who was well established, joked that he was a Broker, and getting broker all of the time. In any event, I figured I might be able to go for a little while just renting the two rooms, but I really had to find a job.

There were a couple of cab companies in Stockton, so I thought I'd go ask—with my driving record in hand—how long I might have to wait before it was clear enough to drive for them. I already knew that I was restricted for nearly three years before I could drive in SF again. It wouldn't hurt to ask, and perhaps a laugh for someone, considering the magnitude of my bad record with the DMV.

So, I went to a local cab company, and met with the owner who seemed to be entertained by the fact that I walked in wearing a suit and tie. It's something that I found made me out of place in Stockton, but I had been doing it all of the time so that I didn't feel like a bum, or get treated like one.

"Oh, I'm still dressed for court," I told him, making a joke of it, and holding out my driving record. "I know it's bad, but I just wanted to get an idea of how long I might have to wait before I could drive a cab in Stockton."

He seemed like the happiest cab company operator that I'd ever met, and a really cool guy; or he was just taken by the oddity of someone wearing a suit and tie walking into his place looking for a job. He took my driving record, and looked at it carefully, as if scrutinizing each of the 27 entries. Then, to my surprise, he acted as if there was nothing wrong with it.

"Looks OK to me," he said, "you've got a valid drivers license. Have you driven a cab before?"

"In San Francisco." I replied.

Instead of the normal total rejection I'd get from my bad record, he acted impressed.

"Do you want to drive a cab here?" he asked.

"Why not?"

"Do cab drivers in San Francisco wear a suit?"

"Sometimes," I said.

"Not here," he advised me. "You walk in when they are expecting a cab driver, but wearing a suit they think you are someone important, and it disrupts the business."

"Well, how can I become a cab driver in Stockton?"

"Can you handle driving the night shift?"

"Of course," I said, not knowing what I was agreeing to.

"Then if you go to the police station and get a temporary permit you can start tomorrow night with cab #79."

I had exited the freeway one day just a few weeks earlier -- wanting to pretend I was entering a whole new world. It was all too easy. Everything seemed to be falling into place in my favor, but I still didn't know anything at all about this town. Suddenly I was driving a cab again. I was about to find out about the whole new world I had entered, the very strange world of Stockton. Driving taxi took a new turn.

...and I'd better drop you off now before I get you into trouble.

Stockton is a crazy place!

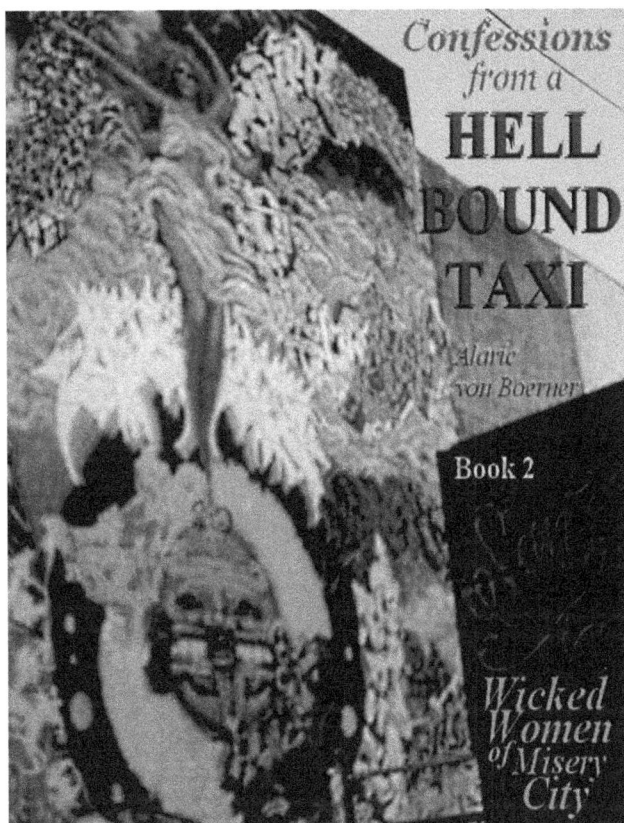

Driver goes through a meatgrinder in BOOK 2.
Take a look at **www.TAXIJAZZ.com**

www.ingramcontent.com/pod-product-compliance
Lightning Source LLC
Chambersburg PA
CBHW021340090426
42742CB00008B/676

* 9 7 8 0 9 8 3 3 8 2 9 1 1 *